DAYS OF THE STEAMBOATS

BY WILLIAM H. EWEN

MYSTIC SEAPORT MUSEUM
1988

HALF TITLE

The Pocahontas *was one of a fleet of side-wheel
steamboats operated by the Old Dominion Line on
lower Chesapeake Bay and the James River. Later
she served as an excursion boat in New York Harbor.*

FRONTISPIECE

The Mississippi steamboat Princess *in this old print
is shown making a night landing at a plantation to
load bales of cotton as well as wood for the fires.*

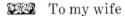 To my wife

CONTENTS

The magnificent Lake Erie steamboat Atlantic
went to the bottom after colliding with the
propeller Ogdensburg *on a dark stormy night.*

IF you had lived back in the nineteenth century, your home probably would have been very near one of America's hundreds of rivers, lakes, and bays. Before there were any railroads or automobiles the waterways were the "highways," and people used them as a means of travel from place to place. Settlements appeared along the shores, and many of these grew into villages, and even cities. From the very earliest days, boats of one kind or another were always to be seen. At the end of the Colonial period, after America had won the war for independence, most of our citizens lived in that part of the country bounded by the Atlantic Ocean, the St. Lawrence River on the north, and the Allegheny Mountains on the west. A great deal of travel, except in the wintertime, was up and down rivers like the Hudson and the Connecticut, and through the sounds and bays along the coast which offered shelter from the stormy waters of the ocean.

Soon many venturesome Americans began to push westward through the wilderness, out onto the great plains and even to the far-off West Coast. In their wanderings they found new rivers and lakes, and many settled beside these waterways. It was not long before the birchbark canoes and dugouts of the Indians began to disappear, and they were replaced by the rafts, flatboats, and poleboats of the settlers. On the Great Lakes, as along the East Coast, sailboats were used to carry passengers and merchandise between east and west, and later, from United States ports to those on the Canadian shores of the Lakes.

Early boatmen depended on the wind, or on river currents to carry them over the waterways. When these were not favorable, bodily strength had to be used. Some boats were paddled or rowed. Others were moved by pushing against the river bottom with long poles. On the Mississippi great rafts floated with the current from the northern reaches of the river all the way down to New Orleans. There they were broken up, and their timbers sold. It would have been impossible to push them back up the river to their starting points. So, it can be seen that travel on the western rivers, except for short distances, was mostly downstream toward the Gulf of Mexico. On the eastern rivers like the Hudson, the currents were not so strong, and the effects of the ocean tides could be felt far upstream. Here wide-bottom sloops and schooners were the types of boats mainly used, and there were hundreds of them in service.

In 1807 an event happened that was to change travel by water completely throughout the entire North American Continent. A steamboat, designed and built by the great inventor, Robert Fulton, began running between New York City and Albany on the Hudson River. There had been other steamboats in American waters before this, but they were mostly experimental. Their builders were not able to find enough support to keep them going. Robert Fulton's steamboat was

Robert Fulton's North River Steamboat *paddling through the Hudson Highlands*

much bigger than any that had been built earlier, and although it was crude in many ways, it made money, and kept on running. From this first self-propelled vessel on the Hudson came hundreds of other steamboats, big and little. By 1860 there was hardly a bay, lake, or river anywhere in the country that didn't have at least one or two steamers.

Try to imagine for a moment that it is the year 1870. The Civil War is over, and the United States is hard at work building itself into a great industrial nation. It is a hot, peaceful summer's day and you are sitting by the bank of the Mississippi. The only movement is on the surface of the river as the swift current carries the muddy water southward. As you look down the river beyond the bend you see a cloud of thick black smoke. The upper part of it spreads out and hangs motionless in the warm lazy air. The base of the column of smoke moves closer and closer, and soon, over the tops of the cottonwood trees you can see two tall black smokestacks. Just back of these appear steady, regular puffs of snow-white vapor. Then you hear a sound, *chow! chow! chow!* the exhaust steam shooting upward through the escape pipes of a big steamboat. Onward, around the bend she comes, a white side-wheeler, looking just like a stately palace moving up the river. You soon hear a new sound, the beat of her paddles as the huge revolving wheels turn the water into foam. As she approaches the point where you are, you jump up and wave wildly, hoping the pilot will see you. He does, and in a moment the deep note of the steam whistle sends shivers up and down your spine. The

Grand Stairway

Most of the big night boats in the East had grand staircases leading from the quarter-deck to the main saloon.

steamboat passes, and is soon out of sight around the next bend. The waves created by her movement through the water slap against the riverbank, then all is quiet again. You sit down to wait for the next steamboat, knowing that it will be along soon. In those days there was a steady parade of them up and down the river at all hours of the day and night.

If you were sitting by the Hudson River instead of the Mississippi the scene would be almost the same. But the steamboat would be quite different. She would be longer in proportion, and lower than the Mississippi steamer. Her bow would be long and sharp, rather than broad and blunt. Her low-pressure condensing engine, which used the steam over and over, would not have any chuffing exhaust pipes, and her paddle wheels would be turned by a "walking beam," an iron device like a huge seesaw swaying up and down above the topmost deck.

Even more exciting than watching a steamboat was a trip on one. Imagine that your parents are taking you aboard one of the big Hudson River night boats for a trip to Albany. You walk from the pier shed across the gangplank onto what is called the quarter-deck of the steamer. This is toward the stern, and back of the big side paddle wheels. All is confusion as hundreds of other passengers hurry aboard and make their way up the grand staircase to find their staterooms on the decks above. You and your parents follow them after stopping at the purser's office for the keys, and finding a porter to carry the bags. At the top of the stairs you turn, walk forward, and

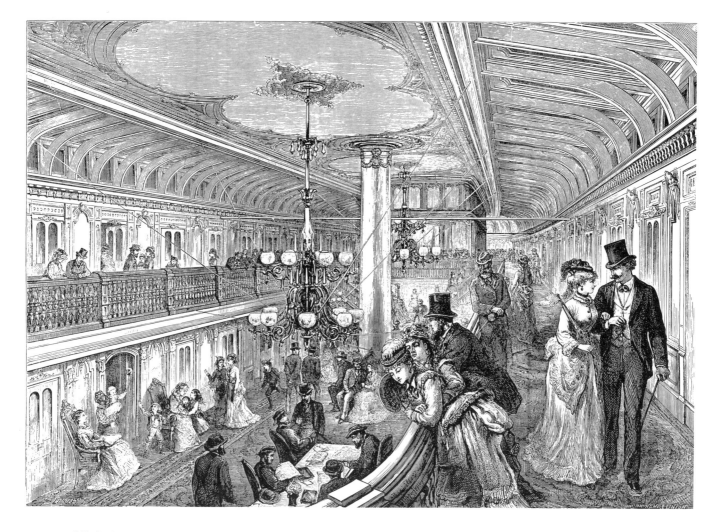

Night boats on the Hudson River and Long Island Sound had wonderful two-story "grand saloons" where passengers congregated before going to bed in their staterooms or berths.

Some passenger staterooms were light and airy like this one, but most were small and had berths instead of regular beds.

find yourself in a huge hall two decks high. This is the "grand saloon." It is lighted by great gas-burning glass chandeliers hanging from the ceiling. There's a thick carpet underfoot and lots of big armchairs. People are already sitting in many of these, reading. Others are walking along the galleries on the deck above, stopping now and then to watch the activity down where you are.

You find your stateroom, and while bags are being unpacked, the deep sound of the whistle announces that the steamer is about to sail. Your parents give you permission to run back to the main deck, and you arrive there just in time to see the gangplank pulled onto the dock as the lines are cast off. Suddenly there's the sound of a big gong from the engine room, and a shudder runs through the steamer as the wheels begin to turn. Slowly at first, then faster and faster she pulls away from the pier. You run forward through the passageway alongside the engine room to watch the engineer raising and lowering the steam valves with a starting bar in order to get the engine up to running speed. Up and then down he pushes, while the big valves click and the steam hisses. Suddenly he steps forward and adjusts a lever. The rocker arms on each side drop into place with a clank, and the big engine is "hooked up." The engineer can now sit down and rest, but he must be on the alert for the sound of the gong when the pilot signals "slow" or "stop."

You leave the engine room with its smell of steam and hot oil, and go back to the quarter-deck. As you stand by the rail now, the water seems to be rushing past. A track of foam stretches out from the paddle wheels almost as far as you can see. You climb from deck to deck, exploring the steamboat, and soon find yourself on the hurricane deck. Standing close to the rail, you can see far up and down the river, and when you look straight down at the water the height is scary. Night is coming on, and the Palisades on the west side of the river are casting long shadows. You watch the officers in the pilothouse turning the steering wheel, and you wonder whether they will be able to see very far ahead when it really gets dark. Back down you go to find your parents and to have dinner. Later on you climb into your berth, and listen to the sounds of the steamboat for a long time before dropping off to sleep.

Steamboat Commonwealth. *The scale drawing on the left shows a Long Island Sound steamboat when seen head-on. Notice how narrow the hull is compared to the width on deck. Paddle wheels are clearly seen, as are the cables and "hog frames" that helped keep the super-structure from sagging. The cut-away view on the right shows how the boilers and paddles wheels were placed. The heavy, upright timbers in the middle of the steamer formed the "gallows frame" that supported the walking beam.*

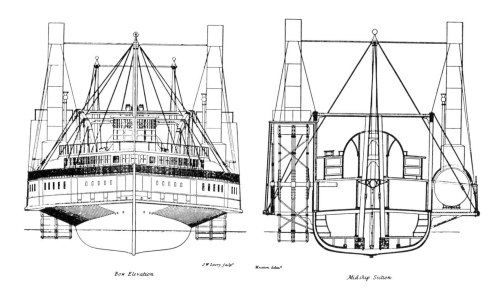

Bow Elevation.

J W Lowry *sculp*

Mazton *delin*

Midship Section.

The little steamboat Sabino, *last coal-burning passenger steamboat in the U.S., runs trips up and down the Mystic River in Connecticut. She is operated and well-maintained by Mystic Seaport Museum.*

Yes, a trip on a steamboat was an experience never to be forgotten. Now almost all of these wonderful vessels are gone forever. In a period of only about 150 years they came into being, became the principal means of moving people and goods throughout our new country, then faded away as the railroads and automobiles took their place.

The very earliest steamboats of the East Coast were built like the sailing ships of those days. In fact, they were a crossbreed, and many carried sails to help them along when the wind was blowing in the right direction. As builders learned more about the behavior of these new vessels they improved them, and soon created a type of boat that never had been seen before. Ocean-going sailormen wanted it understood that these new-fangled craft were not in the same class with their great sailing ships, and the less they had to do with steamboats the better they liked it. Steamboat men, on the other hand, knew they had something exciting to offer travelers, and they featured the term "steamboat" in their advertising in the newspapers and everywhere else. The name became a part of the language, and it meant a very specific kind of vessel.

Steamboats in different parts of our country did not look alike, by any means. Some had side paddle wheels, some had stern wheels, some even had propellers. Some were long and low. Others were short and tall. Some were giants, and many were hardly bigger than motorboats. Regardless of what they looked like, they had one thing in common that made them different from other vessels. Their decks were all constructed above the hull, and in most cases extended out over the water on either side. On many side-wheelers the hull was long and narrow, but the decks above it extended out so far that these steamboats looked very broad when coming toward you or going away. This kind of construction is very different from that of the ocean steamship, where all the decks are entirely inside the hull line. Steamboats were almost always painted white, and with their tall smokestacks, made a very grand appearance. Inside they were often even more impressive, as described earlier. Some, especially those on the Hudson River, were very fast. A few of these could steam along at nearly twenty-five miles an hour. Others, particularly the freight boats, were very slow. Quite a number of steamboats lived long and useful lives. Others blew up, burned, or sank when they were new. Millions of people traveled safely on steamboats, but other thousands lost their lives in accidents throughout the steamboat age.

Hudson River side-wheel steamboat Alexander Hamilton *made her last trip on Labor Day 1971. She was the last of a great fleet of Hudson River vessels, and the last steamboat on the River.*

HOW STEAMBOATING BEGAN

 IT was the morning of August 17, 1807. New York City, a busy place even in those days, was humming with its regular business activity. But this day was different from others. There was something special going on, and many of the citizens knew it. From a dock on the North, or Hudson River near the state prison a great deal of smoke could be seen. Word was out that Robert Fulton at last was going to try to run his North River steamboat all the way to Albany and back. Most people laughed when they talked about it. The idea was crazy, they thought.

Fulton, however, knew better. He had already made several trial trips in the steamboat, and was sure she could make the planned voyage if the machinery did not break down. He had even invited a number of his friends and acquaintances to go along. Some suddenly found that they were ill, or had to be out of town, and sent their apologies. Finally there were only twenty-four people brave enough to march past the laughing crowds down by the dock, and go aboard the steamboat. By noontime the shore was lined with people, and the activity aboard the vessel increased. Smoke poured from the tall thin stack. Fulton could be seen checking over the exposed machinery which stood above the deck, and while he worked the crowd shouted things that would be called wisecracks today.

At one o'clock the lines were cast off, and the crude engine began to grind and clank. The uncovered paddle wheels turned, and began to throw showers of spray into the air. The steamboat moved out into the river, and as she headed her bow upstream a mighty shout went up from the crowd. They realized now that they had been wrong in thinking that the steamer would not work, and they gave Fulton cheer after cheer. Then they stood watching as the vessel moved north, and finally became a speck in the distance. The excitement of the men and women on shore was nothing compared to the feelings of those on board. The engine turned hour after hour without stopping, and as New York disappeared from view Fulton relaxed somewhat. His

Paragon *was Robert Fulton's third steamboat on the Hudson. She was built in 1811 and ran until she struck a rock and sank in 1821.*

guests talked about the wonderful experience they were having. They returned the hails from passing sloops and schooners, and enjoyed the scenery.

By the time the mountainous part of the river, known as the Highlands, was reached it was dark. The deck and the surrounding water were lighted by the flames and sparks from the wood burned under the boiler. The steamboat appeared very much like a column of fire moving up the river, and she attracted the attention of many a farmer along shore. Some who had not heard about the vessel were frightened. So were the crews of the sloops who watched this weird sight bearing down upon them. They may have been reassured when they heard the steamboat's passengers singing, but they gave the strange craft a wide berth just to be safe.

On through the night the steamboat paddled. By dawn she was well into the upper river, and as she passed the little villages along the way people rushed out to see her. At one o'clock, just twenty-four hours after leaving New York, she arrived at Clermont, the estate of Chancellor Robert R. Livingston, Fulton's partner. Many of the guests went ashore with Fulton, while the steamer anchored until next morning.

Promptly at nine o'clock on August 19th, the steamboat moved out into the channel off Clermont, and resumed the trip to Albany. By late afternoon citizens of the capital city could see the smoke as she made her way through the islands of the upper river. At five o'clock she arrived at the landing place where crowds of curious people had waited. As she tied up for the night the happy passengers went ashore realizing that they had taken part in one of the great events in history. Fulton was delighted with the success of the trip, and the steamboat's chief engineer was so relieved that he went to a waterfront tavern and became thoroughly drunk. His condition was so bad that he had to be left behind when the steamer sailed for New York next morning.

This first successful steamboat has usually been called *Clermont*. However, there is nothing to prove she ever carried that name. Fulton referred to her as "the Steamboat." In her very first custom-house papers she was called the *North River Steamboat*. No one really knows how she came to be miscalled the *Clermont*, but this mistake has been carried on through the years and right up to the present time. When she first appeared on the river she was 133 feet long and very narrow. Later she was lengthened to 150 feet and made somewhat wider. Her engine was built in England by James Watt, and with its copper boiler, was sent across the ocean to New York on a sailing ship.

The *North River Steamboat* ran successfully on the Hudson for seven years. By the time she was broken up in 1814, Robert Fulton had designed and built several new and improved steamboats, and these took her place on the Albany line.

Most early eastern steamboats carried sails to help them along when the wind was right. This is the Hudson River steamboat Hope.

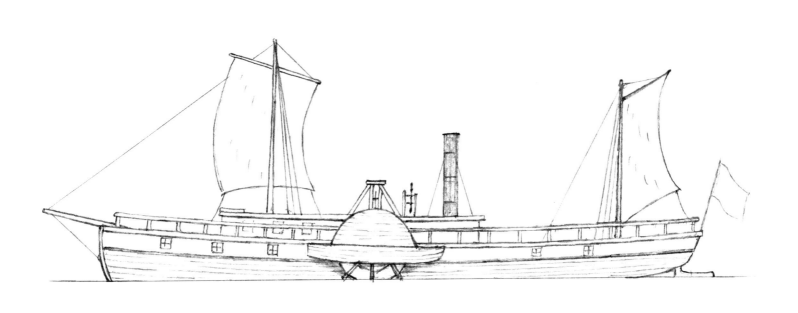

The New Orleans *sailed from Pittsburgh for New Orleans in 1811.*
Built by Nicholas Roosevelt on plans by Robert Fulton, she
was the very first steamboat to navigate the western rivers.

ROBERT FULTON'S first steamboat, as we have seen, was built for the Hudson River. But the great inventor had much bigger ideas in mind. He thought that steamboats would be most useful to the young nation on the great rivers of the West: the Mississippi, the Ohio, the Missouri, and all of the others that flowed into these main streams.

In 1810 Fulton and his partner, Chancellor Livingston, sent Nicholas Roosevelt to the little backwoods city of Pittsburgh where he started a six-months' voyage to explore the Ohio and Mississippi rivers all the way to New Orleans. Mr. Roosevelt, who was a distant relative of our two famous presidents, had been working with steamboats for a number of years. He had a large flatboat built, and with his wife and a crew of experienced boatmen, set off on a dangerous voyage through wild country. Their vessel, like other flatboats, was just a huge watertight box that drifted with the current. Once in a while when the wind was right they might use a sail, but most of the time it was the flow of the river that carried them along. The crew used "sweeps," which were like giant oars, to keep the boat from running aground. The travelers saw many Indians during the long trip, for this part of the country was still largely wilderness.

Finally, New Orleans was reached, and the Roosevelts returned to the East Coast on a sailing vessel. Robert Fulton was so impressed by Roosevelt's report that a new company was set up to build a steamboat for the lower Mississippi.

In 1811 Roosevelt returned with his wife to Pittsburgh, and construction began on a 116-foot-long steamboat designed by Fulton. It was hard work. Men were sent into the nearby forests to cut trees, and these were sawed by hand into planks for the hull and decks. Most of the machinery was carried overland in pieces and put together on board the steamer. Several times during the construction floods raised the level of the river and nearly floated the vessel before she was ready.

Toward the end of the summer the work was finished, and in September the steamer, christened *New Orleans*, left her birthplace never to return. Rivermen said, "You may get to New Orleans, but there you'll stay. No steamboat can move upstream against the current." They were wrong, as we will see later. On board the *New Orleans* when she sailed were the Captain, an engineer and a pilot, six deckhands, two women servants, a cook, a waiter, and a huge Newfoundland dog named Tiger. Mr. and Mrs. Roosevelt were also included in the group, of course. Their friends in Pittsburgh thought it was terrible that Roosevelt would risk his wife's life on such a trip. They tried hard to get her to stay behind. She laughed at their fears, and went along in spite of the warnings.

The *New Orleans* arrived at Cincinnati four days after leaving

Pittsburgh, and the whole town came out to greet the travelers. After taking on fuel, the steamer left for Louisville, further down the Ohio River. As she steamed away the people waved goodbye, saying much the same things as the Pittsburgh natives. They did not expect to see the vessel again.

In the year 1811 many strange things happened. The air during the summer was heavy, smoky, and hard to breathe. A great comet had been visible in the night sky for some time, and superstitious people felt that something terrible was about to happen. They thought their fears were realized when the *New Orleans* arrived at Louisville. It was after dark, and in the light of a full moon the steamer came about and dropped anchor. With the engines stopped, steam pressure built up, and suddenly, with a rumble and a roar, she began to blow off steam. Never had such a noise been heard in this backwoods country. People tumbled out of bed, scared to death. The first thought of many was that the comet had fallen out of the sky and into the river. They rushed to the waterfront, and were amazed to see the steamboat at anchor out in the stream. Next day Louisville celebrated the great event, and the Roosevelts were honored at a dinner.

To repay his hosts for their kindness Mr. Roosevelt invited them aboard the *New Orleans* for a meal the next day. While they were seated at the table in the cabin the steamer suddenly began to shake and move. The guests jumped up and ran out on deck, fearing that the vessel had pulled her anchor and was drifting into the great falls just below the town. What they found out was that Mr. Roosevelt had quietly ordered the engines started. The *New Orleans* was heading upstream against the current! They had said it couldn't be done, and he had proved they were wrong. After traveling several miles up the river the steamer returned to Louisville and let off its happy passengers.

The Roosevelts now faced one of the greatest dangers in the entire trip—getting the steamboat past the rocky rapids called the Great Falls of the Ohio River. There had been very little rain, and the river level was low. It was decided to wait for higher water so there wouldn't be so much chance of wrecking the *New Orleans* on the rocks. This delayed the voyagers for several weeks, and while they waited it was decided to steam back upriver to Cincinnati. The residents of that city couldn't believe their eyes. Here was the steamboat they said wouldn't ever come back. Her arrival started another celebration which lasted for several days.

Finally, more water flowed into the river, and the *New Orleans* was made ready for the dash through the falls. Extra pilots were hired, and men were stationed on her forward deck to signal any quick changes in steering that might be needed. Full steam was gotten up, and the paddle wheels turned faster and faster. With the added speed of the current the *New Orleans* fairly raced into the foaming, rushing water ahead. In the midst of the rapids she bounced around like a cork, but managed to avoid the big jagged rocks on either side. In a few minutes she was safe and sound in the calm water below the falls.

The crowds that had gathered to watch the great event gradually dwindled away as people headed for home. But, no sooner had the steamboat gone past the falls than the whole countryside began to tremble and shake. A great earthquake had started! The people remembered the comet, and were more sure than ever that awful things were in store for them. In some ways they were right. The earthquakes continued for days, and many people lost their lives or their homes as the earth heaved and buckled.

As the *New Orleans* headed out of the Ohio River and into the Mississippi, the earth shocks could hardly be felt through the vibration of her machinery. But when she stopped for the night or landed for fuel, those on board clearly felt the tremors. At times it was almost bad enough to make them seasick as the steamboat rocked and rolled. When she reached the town of New Madrid, Louisiana, it was found that many homes and other buildings had been swallowed up by the earth in great chasms that had opened and then closed. Homeless, frightened people begged to be taken on board, but Mr. Roosevelt had to refuse. They just couldn't be accommodated on the steamer.

In the lower river a great flood had spread across the land. The travelers watched big chunks of the riverbank fall into the stream, sometimes carrying along huge trees. It was hard to find a safe place to tie up each night. On one occasion the steamer was moored at the foot of a large island. Next morning the island had disappeared, and the *New Orleans* was anchored in the middle of a

wide expanse of water. Floating trees, logs, and debris were everywhere. Every now and then rafts, flatboats, and keelboats would be passed. Nobody had much to say. Everyone appeared quiet and worried. Indians in their canoes showed up from time to time. Some seemed to want to get close to the steamer, while others paddled away as fast as they could go. At one place a war canoe filled with yelling braves came out from shore and raced the *New Orleans*. There were more Indians in it than there were crew members aboard the steamboat. It was feared for a time that the savages would try to come aboard, but they were soon left behind. The Indians called the *New Orleans* "Penelore," which meant "Fire Canoe." Many of them thought it had caused the dull, heavy air and the earthquakes. For years afterward the members of several tribes wouldn't set foot on a steamboat. They thought the whole idea was the work of evil spirits.

With the flood waters and the changing landscape, the pilot of the *New Orleans* became lost in the lower river. Directions were asked of passing boatmen, but even the experienced navigators were confused. Finally, by following the main current, the steamer found her way again and reached the city for which she had been named. Her life from then on was not nearly as exciting, for she went into regular service carrying passengers and freight between New Orleans and Natchez on the lower river. In 1814 she met her end above Baton Rouge when a stump punctured her hull and she sank. She had proved that steamboats could navigate the western rivers, and for that she will always be remembered.

Partly sunken trees called "snags" made it very hard to run steamboats on the western rivers. This 1835 painting by Karl Bodmer, a Swiss landscape artist, shows a Missouri River vessel trying to get past hundreds of sunken trees during a period of low water.

STEAMBOATS ON THE HUDSON

FTER the Revolutionary War, as we have mentioned, most of our young country's population was concentrated along the upper part of the Atlantic Coast. Larger towns and cities were all located on the many bays, rivers, and harbors, and travel from one place to another was usually by stagecoach or small sailing vessel. If a man wanted to make good speed through the country-side he would go on horseback. Roads were narrow, dusty in summer, muddy in the rainy periods and when the spring thaws came. Shallow streams were crossed by fording, which meant wading for horses and men and wet wheels for the coaches and wagons. The deeper wider rivers had to be crossed on ferryboats, and these could be anything from small rowboats to large flatboats that would carry one or more stagecoaches. Towns were quite close together, and there were many comfortable roadside taverns where people could have a good meal and a night's rest.

For most of the year the pleasantest way to travel was by sailing vessel, although it was often slower than going overland. When winter's icy blasts came and the rivers froze, the sailboats had to stop running. Many people did not travel at all during the bad seasons, preferring to stay inside close to their fireplaces.

Sailing vessels were mostly small sloops and schooners, and their captains usually were their owners. Some of these men were very bold, often taking their little vessels out into the open ocean. A few sailed as far away as China and Africa. America had no big ships at that time. The British, during the period when they controlled the Colonies, would not allow the building of any large vessels that might compete with their own for trade across the oceans, or that might become warships to threaten their control of the seas. It wasn't until after the Revolution that big naval vessels like the *Constitution* ("Old Ironsides") were built. The famous and beautiful **clipper ships did not come into being until the 1840s and afterward.**

Many men had dreamed of ways to make travel easier and faster throughout the Colonies, and the idea of boats moved by steam power was very much in their minds. Benjamin Franklin considered the possibility. James Rumsey, a gentleman from Virginia, actually built a craft which moved on the jet principle. A steam pump forced a stream of water through a pipe at the stern. While this boat was not very successful, it was really the granddaddy of today's jet boats, planes and rockets. John Fitch, a gloomy, poverty-stricken New Englander, became obsessed with the thought of steamboats, and he carried on endless experiments. His plans developed far enough that he was able to get others to put up the money for three steamboats before 1800. All of these operated for a short time on the Delaware River, but their machinery and the mechanical oars and other strange devices used to push them through the water were so crude that all failed.

Fitch and his supporters lost their money, and the poor inventor later committed suicide. When you consider that he had almost no education, and thought out everything he did without any real scientific knowledge of steam engines or their use, Fitch could be called a genius. There were others who experimented with steamboats, but their work in most cases came to a dead end.

It was Robert Fulton who really gave steamboating its start. His *North River Steamboat*, which we described earlier, was not an experiment. Fulton had enough confidence in his plans to build a vessel that would go into regular service on the Hudson River right from the start. When she made her first trip there were no other steamboats running anywhere in North America, and from that summer's day in 1807 there have been steamboats running continuously right down to the present time. Fulton was not the inventor of the steamboat, but his brilliant mind and his self-taught engineering know-how gave steamboating its successful beginning.

From the day that the *North River Steamboat* appeared on the river other men planned to go into the business. They couldn't operate on the Hudson, however, because New York State had given Fulton and Livingston exclusive rights on the great river, and throughout the state as well. John Stevens of Hoboken, New Jersey, a famous engineer and inventor, built a steamboat very much like Fulton's, and launched it in 1808. This boat, called the *Phoenix*, had no place to run near New York, so the next year Stevens sailed it out of New York Harbor, down the coast to Delaware Bay, where it soon went into service between Philadelphia and Trenton on the Delaware River. The *Phoenix* was the first steamboat to venture out into the open sea, and she was the forerunner of the great era of steamboat commerce on the Delaware River and Chesapeake Bay.

Robert Fulton designed a number of other steamboats, and some of these were built and operated after his death in 1815. He invented and built the first double-ended steam ferryboat, a type of vessel that has been used on most of the rivers and bays of the East and West Coasts of North and South America ever since.

In 1824 the Supreme Court of the United States ruled that the special privilege given to the company formed by Fulton and Livingston was unconstitutional. This caused a mad scramble on the part of men who wanted to get into this profitable business right away. New steamboats, big and little, began sliding down the builders' launching ways by the dozens. Soon the waters of the Hudson and of Long Island Sound were dotted with steamboats where only sails had been seen before. People became used to the booming sound of paddle wheels and to the long columns of black smoke that drifted through the air as the steamboats passed. Travel on these new craft became an adventure, and many people tried it just for the novelty. Others were afraid of steamboats, just as many today fear airplanes. Whenever a boiler exploded or a boat caught fire they'd say, "See. We told you those new contraptions aren't safe. They're against all the laws of nature!"

The Hudson became a testing ground for new steamboats. It

was a route of very heavy travel, not only for people between New York and the state capital, Albany, but also for thousands of settlers and immigrants heading for the West. There was lots of money to be made by owners of good steamboats on the 150-mile Hudson River run, and many moved in with dreams of getting rich overnight. Some did, while others went broke because their vessels were not big enough or fast enough. Speed became the important thing, and designers improved their plans until they were turning out real racers. Fulton's first steamboat moved at five or six miles an hour in 1807. By the 1840s some Hudson River boats were steaming along at close to 20 miles per hour. The long racy lines of these vessels and their side-wheel "walking beam" engines became the model for most of the East Coast vessels from then on.

With so many steamboats entering the river trade in the 1840s, things became overcrowded. Owners tried all kinds of dirty tactics to drive each other out of business. A favorite trick was to hire "runners," rough, tough men who would stand on the docks and try to persuade travelers to go aboard their employers' boats instead of the opposition craft. When several steamboats left from the same dock at about the same time the yelling of the runners before sailing was enough to scare the passengers away. Often they would shout insulting remarks at each other, and sometimes they would get into fist fights.

Once the steamboats got under way, things were often worse. There might be races, with safety valves tied down so that steam

WRECK AND DESTRUCTION OF THE STEAMBOAT SWALLOW,
DREADFUL LOSS OF LIFE!!

Representation of the Loss of the Steamboat SWALLOW, on her passage from Albany to New-York, while opposite Athens, on the night of the 7th April, 1845. The boat first struck a large rock, breaking her in two about midships; after which she took fire and immediately sunk. It is supposed that nearly sixty persons lost their lives.

pressure built up and boilers exploded. Occasionally, steamboats would deliberately run into one another, causing a lot of damage.

One night in April 1845 the steamboat *Swallow* left Albany for the all-night trip to New York. Two other steamers left at the same time and a race began. It was cold and wintry, and as the vessels neared the city of Hudson a heavy snowstorm made it impossible to

Wreck of the Hudson River steamboat Swallow *in April 1845.*

33

see ahead. The *Swallow's* captain, thinking that he knew the channel well enough, kept his boat going at full speed. Suddenly there was a tremendous crash. The steamer had run head on into a small rocky island. With her keel broken, and water pouring into the splintered hull, she began to sink. Soon fire began to spread through her cabins. Screaming passengers in their nightclothes began jumping overboard into the icy water. There were about 40 lives lost.

But even a terrible accident like this didn't stop the reckless racing. It took an even worse disaster to shock the people and to get the Congress of the United States to pass laws that ended the worst dangers. In 1852 the steamboat *Henry Clay* left Albany on July 28th in a race with another steamer called the *Armenia*. All through the early morning in the narrow channel of the upper Hudson they steamed along almost side by side. Once they actually came together with a crash. Passengers were frightened, and several women fainted. Men tried to get the officers of the *Henry Clay* to stop racing, but they paid no attention. At one point they even tried to push the *Armenia* into shallow water where she would run aground. Toward the middle of the afternoon when the *Henry Clay*, still going at top speed, was almost in sight of New York, fire broke out near the middle of the vessel. Fanned by a strong river breeze, the blaze gained headway fast. In a matter of minutes the whole midship section was a mass of flames. The pilot headed the *Henry Clay* for the east bank of the river, which she soon struck at full speed. Her bow went up against the bank, while the stern still sat in deep water. Since most of the passengers,

including many women and children, were on the after end of the steamer, they had a choice of jumping overboard and possibly drowning, or burning to death. The vessel burned to the water's edge in a very short time, and when it was all over more than 80 people had lost their lives.

Steamboating wasn't all danger and accidents. On a good boat in fine weather there was lots to enjoy. People preferred the boats to the smoky, rattling railroad trains that by this time were chugging along the east shore of the river. Each new steamboat seemed to be bigger and finer than ever. Great night boats with comfortable staterooms and huge two-story "grand saloons" made their appearance. Day boats began running on regular timetables like railroad trains, and it surprised some passengers to see a captain standing at the gangplank with his watch in hand, waiting for the exact leaving time before ordering the lines cast off from the dock.

It was in 1861 that the most famous Hudson River steamboat of all began her career. She was named the *Mary Powell*, but she came to be called "Queen of the Hudson." Her lines were beautiful, and she was very fast. Her owners always kept her in spotless condition, and she became known as a "family boat." Her regular run for most of her 60 years on the river was between Rondout, which is the port of Kingston, and New York City. She made the round trip of about 180 miles between these two points every weekday. Only once did the *Mary Powell* have a serious accident. One summer afternoon she was going north in the area of the river known as the "Gorge." The stream is narrow at that point, and steep, rocky mountains are on both sides. It is an area noted for its sudden, violent storms and wind squalls. One of the worst of these in memory hit the *Mary Powell* that afternoon. She was tumbled about, pelted by heavy rain, and for a moment appeared almost to be sucked into the air. By the time her pilot had gotten her under control both of her smokestacks had been blown over. In spite of this she sailed on up the river, made the regular landings, and arrived at her home port nearly on time.

Millions of people traveled on the *Mary Powell* through the years. Most were just ordinary citizens, but many famous people trod her decks, too, including governors and presidents. When she made her last regular trip in 1917, articles were carried in newspapers all over the country, and in magazines. People living along the Hudson actually broke down and cried just as if they had lost a dear friend.

Many other well-known steamboats came after the *Mary Powell*. There were the big Day Line steamers, *Hendrick Hudson* and *Washington Irving*, both over 400 feet long. Between them they could carry a total of 11,000 passengers. The beautiful *Robert Fulton* of the Day Line was the last steamboat on the river to have a walking beam engine. The Albany Night Line also built several giants: the *Adirondack;* the *C. W. Morse;* and the *Berkshire*, largest river steamer ever built in the world. All of these were side-wheelers like most of

Hudson River Night Line side-wheeler Berkshire *was the biggest river steamboat ever built. She ran between New York and Albany from 1913 to 1937. During World War II she was towed to Bermuda and became a barracks for war workers.*

Hendrick Hudson *was a big popular steamboat of the Hudson River Day Line. She had one of the largest passenger licenses ever issued and could carry over 5,000 people. Her speed was 23-25 miles per hour.*

the Hudson River boats down through the years. There were a few propeller steamboats on the river at various times, but never a sternwheeler.

The Hudson is usually a quiet river. The two greatest natural dangers steamboatmen had to face were fog and ice. During a cold winter the surface of the river would freeze solid, and no ordinary steamboat could break its way through without great damage to the hull and paddle wheels. During the days of the old wooden boats many were sunk when the ice cut through their hulls. Others were frozen in, and couldn't move until warm weather caused the ice to break up. Fog appears on the river now and then, especially in the spring and fall, and over the years it caused many steamboats to collide or run aground. A moving vessel in fog is required by law to blow its whistle at regular intervals. There have been captains on the Hudson who knew every foot of the shoreline so well that they could tell exactly where they were, even in the thickest fog by the echoes of the whistle against the shore. Others relied on the familiar sounds of dogs barking, and similar things they had heard during their many trips.

Hundreds of steamboats sailed the Hudson over the years, but there are none left today. The last was the Day Line side-wheeler *Alexander Hamilton*. She was 47 years old when she stopped running in 1971, but she could still steam along at nearly 25 miles per hour in her last days.

The early Long Island Sound steamer New York *was said by*
Charles Dickens to look like a London floating bathhouse.

NEW YORK CITY has been a center of shipping since the days of the early Dutch settlers. To the north is the Hudson River, a great water highway, and to the east, toward New England, Long Island Sound extends for nearly a hundred miles. The Sound is a very large body of water, but even so it is much more protected than the open ocean. For years it was the favorite route for steamboats and ships sailing between New York, Boston, and other ports in New England. Near New York the Sound becomes very narrow as it flows into what is called the East River. This is really not a river at all; it is a strait connecting the Sound with New York Harbor and the ocean. The water flows through the East River at a good speed, first in one direction, then, as the ocean tide changes, in the opposite direction.

At a point on the Long Island shore called Astoria the East River makes a sharp turn to the east, and becomes very narrow. This spot is known as Hell Gate, and its reputation for dangerous currents is well deserved. In earlier times, when steamboats first began running, no vessel had gone through Hell Gate against the tide. The steamboat *Connecticut*, built in 1816, was the first to make it, but she had to get up full steam and try three times before getting through. If she had failed in the last effort, she might have been wrecked on the jagged rocks around which the water surged. The *Connecticut* was followed by other steamboats with more powerful engines, but they all had trouble getting through Hell Gate, too. Finally, government engineers blew up most of the rocks with dynamite, and made Hell Gate a safer place to navigate.

In spite of the dangers in going from New York City into Long Island Sound, many steamboats began running to cities like Bridgeport, Hartford, New Haven, and New London. Some even went as far as Providence, which is up at the head of Narragansett Bay. To reach this point they had to pass out of the eastern end of Long Island Sound, and go into the open ocean around Point Judith. This was dangerous, and the high waves often made passengers seasick. Hardly any of the early steamboats sailed all the way from New York to Boston because they would have to go much further in the Atlantic —all the way around Cape Cod. Since most of the travel east and west was between New York and Boston, several steamboat lines worked out an arrangement in which they took their passengers to places on the Connecticut coast, or to Providence, where people would leave the steamboats and take stagecoaches the rest of the way. Later on, railroad lines were built from Boston to these steamboat landings, and the trip became a lot quicker. Many fine fast steamboats were built for Long Island Sound. One of them, the *Metropolis*, came out in 1854, and she had a cylinder so big that a horse and wagon could be driven through it. As on the Hudson, the Sound steamboats often

Elm City *ran to New Haven from New York.*
You can clearly see the truss called
a "hog frame" rising above her decks.

The Fall River Line steam-boat Pilgrim *came to be known as the "Iron Monarch of Long Island Sound."*

raced, but because there was more room in these wide waters there were not as many accidents from this dangerous business.

The most famous steamboat line on the Sound began in 1847 with a route from Fall River, Massachusetts to New York. This company, the Fall River Line, started its business with two substantial steamboats and, when it gave up service 90 years later in 1937, it had a fleet of four of the biggest side-wheelers ever seen. One of these was the great *Priscilla*, a favorite with New England travelers for more than 40 years. The *Priscilla* had several accidents and many other adventures during the years she ran, but she always came through without serious consequences.

One night in July 1924 she had left Newport, Rhode Island and was moving carefully through a thick fog on her way to New York. Suddenly her radio operator heard an SOS. The Eastern Steamship Line's new *Boston* had been rammed in the fog by a tanker, and was sinking! Passengers were abandoning ship. Captain Fred Hamlen of the *Priscilla* estimated that the *Boston* was about 50 miles away from his own position. The *Priscilla* had almost entered the eastern end of Long Island Sound, and the sinking *Boston* was far astern. No time to lose! Orders were given to the engineer on duty to give her full speed ahead.

Swinging in a wide half circle, the *Priscilla* started her race to the scene of the accident. With her whistle blowing every couple of minutes, the big steamboat went as fast as she had ever gone before. It was after midnight, but several passengers awoke and came out on deck to see why they were going at such a clip. Crew members explained, but the passengers were worried. "What if we hit something in this fog?" said one. "We wouldn't stand a chance." On raced the *Priscilla* through Block Island Sound, her big paddle wheels beating the water into a track of foam that stretched out for a mile behind. Whistles of other steamers were heard in the distance. The Fall River Line's eastbound steamer from New York, the great *Commonwealth*, had also picked up the SOS and was speeding after the *Priscilla*.

Captain Hamlen had plotted his course perfectly. One hour and fifty minutes after starting the voyage of mercy, the bell on the tanker *Swift Arrow*, which had rammed the *Boston*, was heard. The damaged passenger steamship was still afloat, but leaking badly. Most of her passengers were either on board the *Swift Arrow* or bobbing around in lifeboats. They felt much safer when they saw the lights of the big white steamboat close at hand. Over 300 of them were picked up and taken aboard the *Priscilla* for a safe trip to New York.

The Fall River Line steamer Providence *blows a salute at Mt. Hope Bridge over Narragansett Bay. The foaming track from her paddle wheels stretches far back into the distance.*

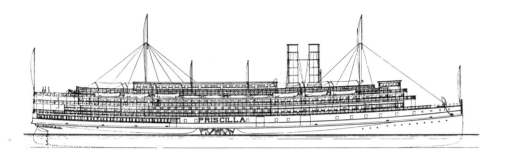

Scale drawing of the famous Fall River Line side-wheeler Priscilla. *She was a favorite of travelers to and from New England for more than 40 years.*

At first nobody knew what to do about the *Boston*. She was a brand-new steamship, and if she sank it would be a great loss. The problem was solved by Captain E. R. Geer of the *Commonwealth*. His steamer had arrived on the scene shortly after the *Priscilla*. The *Commonwealth* moved in slowly until she was alongside of the *Boston*, and the two vessels were lashed together with heavy ropes. The huge side-wheeler towered over the smaller steamship, which had already settled low in the water. Slowly, the *Commonwealth*'s wheels began to turn as she headed in the direction of Newport in the thick fog.

Captain Geer soon found that the *Boston*'s steel hull and superstructure were affecting his compass. He couldn't tell whether or not they were steering in the right direction, so he sent a radio message to another Fall River Liner, the *Plymouth*, which was nearby. He asked Captain Robinson of that steamer to lead the way, and to tell them how to proceed by whistle signals. In this way the strange procession headed for the sheltered waters of Narragansett Bay—two side-wheelers and a wounded steamship.

There was still great danger, however. If the *Boston* started to go to the bottom she might very well pull the *Commonwealth* down with her. To guard against that, members of the steamboat's crew were told to stand by the lines tying the two craft together. Each man had an ax ready, and he knew that the second he heard a certain whistle signal he was to chop through the rope as fast as he could. But the *Boston* didn't sink. Once inside the bay, she was pushed into shallow water where she settled gently in the mud. Salvage vessels soon came, and after they patched the leaks and pumped her out, she was towed away for repairs. In a few weeks she was back in service, thanks to the men and the steamboats of the Fall River Line.

Throughout the 1930s the country was in a business depression. Many companies were losing money. Others had failed. Some just managed to make ends meet. The Fall River Line was one of those having difficulty. In July 1937 the New Haven Railroad, which owned the steamboat company, suddenly decided to end all of its service on Long Island Sound. The *Commonwealth*, *Priscilla*, *Providence* and *Plymouth* were taken to Newport and Providence to await their fate. Soon tugs came to tow them to Baltimore where they were broken up for scrap. As with the *Mary Powell* on the Hudson, hundreds were saddened by the passing of the steamboats they loved. The wonders of the Fall River Line will never be forgotten by those who traveled on its steamers. Today there are no steamboats at all running the length of Long Island Sound. The very last one has followed the Fall River Line into history.

EXCURSION BOATS

AS we have seen, New York was the center of steamboat activity on the Hudson River and on Long Island Sound. It was also the headquarters of hundreds of big and little steamboats engaged in the business of taking people to the many beaches, picnic groves and amusement parks near the city. On a summer's day in years gone by New York Harbor would be crowded with these vessels on the way to Coney Island, Rockaway Beach, Locust Grove on the Sound, or Alpine up the Hudson. Bands would play while passengers danced or just sat by the rail enjoying the harbor sights and the breeze. Many of the steamboats were hired by clubs or special groups, just as buses are hired today. Excursions were fun, except when passengers drank too much. Then fights often started and people would fall overboard. To guard against loss of life, many steamboats towed a man behind in a rowboat. It was his job to cut loose and pick up anyone who landed in the water. Some passengers thought it was fun to throw beer bottles at this poor lifesaver. When that happened he had to pull his boat up under the overhanging stern of the steamer where he couldn't be seen. A lot of the special excursions were for Sunday schools, and the people on those trips were almost always well-behaved.

June 15, 1904 was a day marked for one of the biggest Sunday school outings of all time. The Lutheran churches in the city had chartered the big side-wheel steamboat *General Slocum* to take mothers and children on an outing to Locust Grove up the Sound. There were a few fathers with their families, but for most men it was a day of work. Those who couldn't go thought of the happy time their wives and children would have. It was a fine day, and the *General Slocum*, carrying 1,358 people, headed up the East River into a light breeze. With a band playing and flags flying, she was a great sight. Passengers on ferryboats and other steamers waved as she passed.

She had only gone a short distance up the river when a boy came panting up the steps to the pilothouse crying, "There's a fire!" "Shut up and mind your own business," he was told. Moments later two deck hands found the mate and told him the bad news. The *General Slocum* was indeed afire in a room at the forward end where paint, rags, and oil for lanterns were kept. The crew hadn't had any fire drills, and didn't know what to do. A few of them pulled out a fire hose and tried to get a stream of water on the blaze which was growing bigger by the minute. The hose was old and rotten, and it burst as soon as the water pressure hit it. Life preservers were pulled down from the ceilings of the decks, but they, too, were rotten, and fell apart. By this time the passengers knew the steamer was burning, and they ran screaming about the decks. A few jumped overboard to escape the flames, and soon many others followed. Not many of the women and children aboard knew how to swim, and most of them quickly drowned in the swift East River current. Captain Van Schaick acted like a man in a stupor. Instead of landing immediately somewhere along shore, he kept the *General Slocum* headed up the river into the wind, and at the same speed. The fire soon raged above the topmost deck, and the screams of the passengers could be heard several blocks from the river. Tugboats sounded distress signals, and followed the doomed steamboat. Factory whistles on land began to blow, calling attention to the terrible disaster that was happening. Men ran to the shore and launched rowboats to try to save those in the river. "Stop! Stop!" they shouted. "Why don't they stop her?"

On went the big steamboat through Hell Gate. A few minutes later she was finally run ashore on a little island called North Brother. By this time she was a raging furnace, and her decks were falling in. The captain and all of the crew managed to get off, but their passengers were not so lucky. When the final list of dead and missing was counted up it was found that over a thousand lives had been lost. The whole nation was shocked. President Theodore Roosevelt set up a special investigating commission, and kept in touch with events from the White House. The whole of New York was in mourning for days. People could talk of nothing but the *General Slocum*. In several parts of the city entire families had been wiped out. Endless funeral processions could be seen slowly crossing the East River bridges to the cemeteries on Long Island.

"Never again will greedy steamboat owners be allowed to send crowds of people out on vessels with rotten fire hose and useless life

The New York Harbor excursion steamboat General Slocum *burned in 1904. More than a thousand passengers died in that disaster.*

preservers," said the Government. From then on steamboats were inspected much more carefully, and people soon lost their fear. The excursion business became good again, and millions of people continued to enjoy pleasant trips on the boats until about the time of World War II. By then most of the excursion steamers were old and tired, and no new ones were built. One by one they stopped running and were laid up or scrapped. After the war, with more and more people owning cars, there was very little interest in steamboat excursions, and so another exciting phase of American life passed into history.

STEAMBOATS ON THE WESTERN RIVERS

TAKE a good map of the United States and look carefully at the rivers in the middle part of our country. There's the Mississippi which starts in the state of Minnesota very near the Canadian border, and flows due south all the way to the Gulf of Mexico. The Ohio River begins at Pittsburgh, Pennsylvania, and flows hundreds of miles to join the Mississippi at Cairo, Illinois. The mighty Missouri, even longer than the Mississippi, commences in Montana close to the Rocky Mountains. It flows through North and South Dakota, Nebraska, Iowa, Kansas, and Missouri, finally running into the Mississippi near St. Louis. Many other rivers, both from the East and West, flow into the "Father of Waters," as the Mississippi is called. In fact, on the map it looks like the trunk of a great tree with branches spreading out in all directions. The waters of this great river system come from 25 states; from New York on the East to Montana on the West. This is the heartland of our country, and it was the goal of many of the early settlers.

We have seen how steamboating began on these western rivers with the first trip of Robert Fulton's little steamer, the *New Orleans*. She was soon followed by other boats designed by Fulton: the *Vesuvius*, *Aetna*, and *Buffalo*. As soon as people were convinced that these vessels were practical, and could go upstream against the current, there was a stampede to get into the business just as there had been on the Hudson earlier. One of the first to get started was Captain Henry M. Shreve. He believed as Fulton did that steamboats were just the thing to open up the West, but he did not think Fulton's vessels were suitable for the rivers. In 1815 Captain Shreve designed and built a steamboat the way he thought it should be done. This vessel, called the *Washington*, was launched into the Ohio River at what is now Wheeling, West Virginia. While Fulton's boats sat deep in the water, the *Washington* floated like a flat board. Her engine operated on high-pressure steam and developed more power for its weight than the heavier, low-pressure engines in the Fulton steamers. The boilers, instead of being placed in the hold, were set up on the main deck. On the 24th of September, 1816, the *Washington* went through the falls of the Ohio River and steamed to New Orleans. Later, she returned to the Ohio just below the falls, and in 1817 made a second trip to New Orleans. It took her about 45 days to make a round trip. The *Washington* and another steamer called the *Enterprise* convinced everyone along the rivers that steamboats could go long distances up the rivers as well as down. Soon shipyards at many places on the Ohio and Mississippi were turning out new steamboats. By the 1830s there were more than 200 vessels chuffing and puffing along with passengers and freight.

Navigating the western rivers was hard work, and it was dangerous, too. Channels shifted from one side of the river to another,

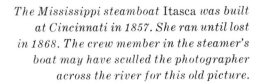
The Mississippi steamboat Itasca *was built at Cincinnati in 1857. She ran until lost in 1868. The crew member in the steamer's boat may have sculled the photographer across the river for this old picture.*

sometimes confusing the pilots so that their boats ran aground. Sand bars appeared in places where the water had been deep. Big trees would fall into the river and get stuck on the bottom, sometimes by the branches and sometimes by the roots. When they stuck up above the water the current often kept them bobbing up and down like a man sawing a log of wood. Rivermen called these "sawyers." Logs and trees that didn't stick up very far were called "snags." Many steamboats were sunk by running into these unexpectedly.

The lower Mississippi River turned and twisted through the countryside like a snake. Some of the bends would take a steamboat right around until for a short time it would be heading back in the direction from which it had come. Big floods often occurred, and the flat land would be covered with water for miles in every direction. Sometimes when the water was high, the river, instead of going around a bend, would shoot straight across the land, creating a new channel. This was called a cut-off. When this happened the old channel around the bend usually dried up. Some people who had built homes near the river soon found themselves far away from it. The Mississippi was full of islands, with the main channel on one side or the other. The side of an island away from the channel would sometimes be deep enough for steamboats, but it might be only wide enough for one boat. These narrow passages were known as "chutes," and pilots sometimes steered their boats through them to save time, especially when they were racing. Often a steamboat in a chute would meet a raft or a flatboat and might have to push it back out of the end where it had entered.

Some of the other rivers were even worse than the Mississippi for steamboats. The Red River, which flows between Texas and Oklahoma and through Louisiana, had so many logs and trees stuck at one place that steamboats could hardly get through. This became known as the "Red River Raft," and it stayed there until the Government sent special boats to clear out the mess. But all of these things didn't stop the early steamboat men from running their vessels. They even found a way to go up through the Great Falls of the Ohio River by pulling the boats with cables fastened to trees.

The early western river steamboats were built very plain, like backwoods farmhouses. Then, to help attract passengers, later boats were made bigger and grander, with lots of fancy carved woodwork and great tall black smokestacks. At first they were mostly side-wheelers, but as the years went on, more and more stern-wheelers were built. Engines and boilers were on the main deck, and the wood or coal used for fuel was stored there. Deck passengers, the poor people who couldn't pay full fare, had to stay on this deck. At night they would try to sleep in the midst of the boxes and bales of freight. The passengers who paid full fare were sent to the upper decks, away from the noise of the engines and the heat of the boilers. They had clean private rooms, and a nice big cabin where they could sit and read and have their meals. To get on or off a steamboat, however, they had to go to the main deck and cross over the gangplank which reached from the bow of the vessel to the riverbank. When the shore was muddy

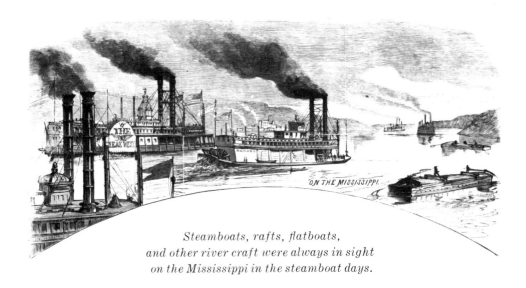

Steamboats, rafts, flatboats,
and other river craft were always in sight
on the Mississippi in the steamboat days.

even the rich passengers might find themselves up to their knees in muck when they hopped off the plank. Someone had the idea of putting the name of a state on the door of each private cabin. The big officers' cabin underneath the pilothouse was called the "Texas" because it was the biggest cabin, and Texas was the biggest state in the Union.

There was so much rivalry in the steamboat business up to the time of the Civil War that pilots and engineers would take terrible risks. Boats would be kept going at top speed when they should have been slowed down. Safety valves would be tied down until the steam pressure in the boilers would bulge them out or explode them. Most of the big steamboats had several boilers in a row, and when all of them blew up at once, big chunks of the steamboat and human bodies would be blown high in the air. This happened so often that people became used to it. Accidents were joked about, especially by those who had never been in one. It was said, for instance, that Mississippi pilots were so skillful in collisions at night that both boats could go to the bottom without waking the lightest sleeper on board. But accidents really were no laughing matter. It was estimated that in the first 40 years of steamboating on the Mississippi over 500 steamboats had been lost by accidents, with several thousand people killed or hurt.

A terrible explosion occurred on board the steamboat *Louisiana* at New Orleans the evening of November 15, 1849. She was just backing out from the wharf with a full load of passengers and freight when all of her boilers burst at once. Houses for blocks around were

A Mississippi River pilot had to know every inch of the waterway both by day and by night. If he didn't, he might easily wreck his steamboat.

shaken as if a bomb had dropped. Two steamers on either side of the *Louisiana* had their upper decks completely wrecked. Big pieces of boiler iron flew through the air and landed on the shore. One fragment cut a mule right in two, then struck a horse and wagon. Both the horse and the driver were killed. Bodies from the *Louisiana* were blown as high as 200 feet in the air, and people on shore were hit by flying pieces of the steamboat and its engines. It was not known exactly how many were killed in this awful blast, but the city of New Orleans was in a state of shock for days afterward.

The most terrible disaster that ever happened to a steamboat anywhere was the explosion of the big Mississippi River boat *Sultana* on the night of April 27, 1865. She was heading upriver with several thousand Union Army soldiers returning from the Civil War. Some were sick and wounded. About 1,600 were lost in the explosion and fire that followed. The wrecked steamer drifted a few miles downstream and sank above Mound City, Illinois. The citizens of that town learned of the disaster only when they heard the cries of survivors floating past on pieces of wood from the vessel.

In spite of the many accidents, most steamers ran until they wore out and had to be broken up. They opened up the West long before the railroads came and took away most of their business.

Steamboats were a great help to our government many times through the years. In the War of 1812 when the British were attacking New Orleans, General Andrew Jackson declared martial law, and he took over Robert Fulton's steamboat *Vesuvius* to help carry troops and supplies. Later on, when the Government sent explorers up the Missouri and Yellowstone rivers, steamboats were used to carry the expeditions. In 1818 a steamboat was built especially for this purpose. She was called the *Western Engineer*. To scare the Indians and to keep them from causing trouble, this vessel was made to look as if she were riding on the back of a sea monster. At the bow there was a huge snake's head with wide-open red mouth. The exhaust steam from the engine hissed out of this opening, making it look as if the monster were really breathing fire. It did frighten the Sioux Indians who had never seen even an ordinary steamboat.

The first steamboat expedition went only about 200 miles up the Missouri, but later ones pushed on all the way to Fort Benton, Montana. On the Yellowstone River explorers managed to run a steamboat as far as a great rock called Pompeys Pillar in southern Montana. This is not far from the place where the Indians massacred General Custer and his men in that famous battle in 1876. In fact, a steamboat called the *Far West* took supplies for Custer's regiment to the mouth of the Little Big Horn River and waited there for news of the fight. It did not take long. A friendly Indian scout on horseback who had been with the troops burst through the bushes at the riverbank with a wild look in his eyes. They took him aboard the steamboat, and through sign language he made them understand that the whole regiment was wiped out and General Custer was dead. Other troops under General Terry had fought the Indians in a different battle some distance from where Custer and his men were. Many of General

Terry's men were killed, but others, including a large number of wounded, escaped. They made their way down along the Big Horn River until they reached the waiting steamboat.

When all the wounded were aboard, the *Far West* turned about in the narrow channel and steamed off as fast as she could.

The stern-wheeler Far West, *on the right in this picture, was one of the most famous Missouri River steamboats. In 1876 she carried supplies for General Custer's troops to the mouth of the Little Big Horn River, and brought the first word of their massacre back to civilization.*

Down the Big Horn she paddled, dodging the rocks and shallows. Captain Marsh had never been down that river before, but he had noticed rocks and other things to watch out for on the trip up. On into the Yellowstone River raced the *Far West*, then down the Yellowstone to the Missouri. At eleven o'clock on the night of July 5th she reached Bismarck, the capital of North Dakota. Steaming along night and day, she had covered 710 miles of treacherous river, all the way from the mouth of the Big Horn in 54 hours.

Up to this moment the rest of the country knew nothing of the terrible fate that had come to General Custer and his troops. There was a telegraph line at Bismarck, and soon the wires were carrying the clicks that spelled out the news. The wounded soldiers were taken off the steamboat and hospitalized, and the *Far West* went back to her duty of carrying troops and supplies. On one of her scouting trips she had famous Buffalo Bill aboard. Years later, after her exciting adventures were over, the *Far West* could be found on the Mississippi running out of St. Louis. In October 1883 she struck a snag and sank, and that ended her famous career.

Most of General Custer's troops were buried on the battlefield where they had fallen. Their leader's body, however, was placed in a coffin and sent east for honored burial at West Point Military Academy on the Hudson. After traveling by steamboat down the Missouri and by train to Poughkeepsie, New York, the General's body was taken aboard the famous Hudson River steamboat *Mary Powell* for the last part of the trip to West Point.

The *Far West* and other steamers on the upper Missouri River were known as "mountain boats." They were smaller and lighter than the big Mississippi boats, and they floated in shallower water. Because of the many sand bars in the Missouri, they needed special equipment to help them get through. Some of them carried big sets of poles up near the bow, and these were known as "grasshoppers" because they looked like the hind legs of those insects you see sailing through the air in the summertime. The grasshoppers worked like a pair of crutches. The main poles would be stuck in the sand a little ahead of the steamer, and at an angle. As the vessel moved ahead the poles would come up straight and lift the bow over the obstructions. Sometimes this had to be done again and again. It made the going very slow until the steamboat reached deeper water. The "mountain boats" had to carry lots of extra food and supplies on their trips because for many years the valley of the upper Missouri was a wild and lonely place. It would take weeks to get to the forts way out west.

By the time the Civil War began there were almost 800 steamboats running on the western rivers. New Orleans had become the main port for steamers on the lower Mississippi, and St. Louis was headquarters for most of the boats on the middle part of the river. Many of the New Orleans boats were on short runs to Natchez, Mississippi or Memphis, Tennessee. They carried great loads of cotton down the river to New Orleans where it was loaded on ocean vessels and then shipped all over the world. Some steamboats made longer trips, going all the way to St. Louis, and up the Ohio River to Louisville, Cincinnati, and Pittsburgh. These voyages took so long that only about five or six could be made in a year. Even so, the boats made lots of money for their owners.

Above St. Louis there were hundreds of miles of river that could be navigated, but there were rapids near the mouth of the Des Moines River and at Rock Island, Illinois. It was quite some time before steamboats managed to get past these obstructions, but they finally did. The upper river business did not grow as fast as trade on the lower Mississippi, but by the 1850s and '60s a large number of vessels were steaming from St. Paul, Minnesota to Galena, Illinois and points in between. Steamboating up north was not at all like that in the lower river. There were not nearly so many twists and turns. Instead of flat land which stretched for miles, there were hills and pretty scenery. The water in the lower river was full of mud and sand, while the upper river was clear. Mud clogged the boilers of the lower river boats, and their engineers had to clean them out every day or so. Most western river steamers had big tanks underneath the boilers, to which they were connected. The mud would settle in these so-called "mud drums," and they would be emptied by opening valves and blowing the silt back into the river under high water pressure. On the upper river steamboats sometimes went for weeks without having their boilers cleaned out.

During the Civil War steamboat owners had a pretty hard time of it. Many of their vessels were taken over and converted to gunboats called "ironclads." This was done by covering up most of the

The Jacob Strader *was an Ohio River steamboat built in 1853.*

superstructure with heavy sheet iron. Great fleets of steamboats were used by both the North and the South to transport troops and supplies and to attack each other's forts along the river. A steamboat that dared to go into enemy territory alone was likely to be seized and lost to its owners forever. Many, many vessels were destroyed in battle during the war, and when it was ended people said that steamboating was finished, too. But it wasn't. Some of the biggest and grandest of the "packets," as they were called, were still to be built. In the 1870s great side-wheelers like the *Thompson Dean*, the *Ed Richardson*, the third *J. M. White*, and the *Grand Republic* appeared. These were so magnificent they were called floating palaces. Nothing like them had ever been seen before, and they gave rivermen hope that the steamboat business would get back to where it was before the war.

It was in 1870 that the greatest steamboat race of all time took place, and while it was going on the attention of people everywhere was on the Mississippi River. The two steamboats involved were the *Robert E. Lee*, owned by Captain John Cannon, and the *Natchez*, owned by Captain Thomas Leathers. These big side-wheelers were very fast, and they competed for freight and passengers on the lower river. Their captains did not like one another, and would not speak when they met. A short while before the race the *Natchez* had made a very fast round trip to St. Louis, and Captain Leathers wanted everyone to believe that he had the fastest boat on the river. Captain Cannon did not like this at all, so he quietly made ready to show his rival that the *Robert E. Lee* could beat the *Natchez*. There were no public announcements that there was going to be a race, but word got around, and soon nearly everyone knew it. Newspapers ran stories, and throughout the civilized world people heard about it by telegraph. Up to the starting day neither captain would admit there was anything special going on. The *Robert E. Lee* was advertised to leave New Orleans for Louisville, and the *Natchez* for St. Louis. However, it was noticed that they were both sailing at about the same time on the same day. This had not happened before.

Captain Cannon planned to take only a small number of passengers for this trip, and he refused to load any freight. This made it unnecessary for the *Robert E. Lee* to stop at her usual landings. Captain Cannon also made arrangements to have barges loaded with coal all ready to be picked up at a number of places along the way. His plan was that these would be tied alongside the *Robert E. Lee*, and

Mississippi steamboat landings were always busy places. Usually the steamers landed at levees, which were paved, sloping riverbanks, or just alongside the shore. Here you can see the big gangplanks which were swung out and lowered by block & tackle so that passengers and freight could be moved on and off.

The Robert E. Lee. *This great Mississippi packet was the winner of the world famous race with the* Natchez *in 1870.*

while she steamed on up the river the coal would be taken aboard. When the barges were empty they were to be cut loose to drift back with the current to where they had been picked up. Finally, he removed fittings and even made structural changes to lighten his steamboat and make it go faster.

On the evening of June 30th the *Robert E. Lee*, with about sixty passengers but no freight, backed away from the wharf at five minutes to five. As she turned and headed up the river, the *Natchez* followed. A number of excursion steamers had taken crowds out earlier in the day, and as the racers went past each of these boats their passengers cheered them on. Whistles were blown, guns were fired, and as night came on bonfires appeared along the shores.

When the *Natchez* had gone a hundred miles the *Robert E. Lee* was still ahead, but only by about six minutes. All through the night the *Lee* stayed in the lead. Passengers and crew on the *Natchez* stayed up most of the night, straining their eyes to try to catch a glimpse of the *Lee*. Both boats went booming past landings like Baton Rouge where crowds stood cheering even though it was after one o'clock. Next day the steamers were in sight of one another from time to time. The *Natchez* made several landings, but the *Lee* only stopped long enough to pick up her coal barges. Late in the afternoon it seemed as though the *Natchez* was gaining, but an accident to part of her engine made it necessary to land for repairs, and a precious half-hour was lost. Every now and then the *Natchez* would seem to gain a little, but then she'd lose time at a landing and would fall back.

The next morning another one of Captain Cannon's advance plans came to light. As the *Lee* steamed along, another steamboat, the *Frank Pargoud*, met her at a prearranged place. The *Pargoud* had on board a hundred tons of pine wood knots to be used under the *Lee's* boilers. As you probably know, these are full of sticky resin, and they make a roaring hot fire. The two boats were lashed together, and the *Frank Pargoud* turned her wheels as fast as the *Lee's*. They proceeded like this, side by side until the fuel had been taken onto the *Lee's* main deck. Then the ropes were untied and the *Frank Pargoud* quickly was left behind.

The *Robert E. Lee's* regular service was from New Orleans to Louisville, Kentucky and the passengers who had gotten aboard before she sailed expected her to leave the Mississippi at Cairo, Illinois for the trip up the Ohio River. It was at that point that they learned again how well Captain Cannon had worked things out. Near the junction of the two rivers, a steamboat called the *Idlewild* came alongside the *Lee*, and most of the Louisville passengers, with bag and baggage, were transferred. The *Lee* then sped on toward St. Louis.

That night about 11 o'clock fog began settling on the river. Soon it became so thick that the shore could not be seen on either side. Captain Cannon ordered the *Lee* slowed until she was just barely moving. No one aboard knew just how close the *Natchez* might be, and it was feared she might slip by. But the *Natchez* was having her troubles. Some miles down the river she, too, was caught in the fog. Captain Leathers made a landing at a wood yard, and was told that

the *Lee* had groped her way past about 25 minutes earlier. He decided to tie up until the fog lifted, thinking that the *Lee* would have to do the same thing. Captain Cannon kept his steamer moving, however, and the *Lee*'s paddles slapped the water very slowly.

Around two o'clock in the morning a breeze came up and blew the fog away. Captain Cannon rang the engine room bell for full speed and the *Lee* was off again like a race horse. At the place where the

In spite of the fact that the Natchez *was beaten by the* Robert E. Lee, *she was said to be one of the finest Mississippi steamboats ever built.*

Natchez had tied up the weather didn't clear until much later. Captain Leathers finally was able to give the order to cast off the lines about 6:30, and the *Natchez* was on her way. It was the Fourth of July and no one had to be at work. Huge crowds lined the shores as the *Robert E. Lee* appeared in the distance below St. Louis. Clouds of black smoke poured out of her stacks, and she plowed up a big wave as she rapidly approached the city's waterfront. Waiting steamboats loaded with passengers began to blow their whistles. Cannons boomed. Cheer after cheer went up from the crowds on shore and on the many waiting vessels. On came the *Lee*. She raced past the landings and went a little way up the river where she turned and came back to tie up. The crowds went wild. Hundreds went aboard the steamer. Captain Cannon was the great hero of the day. The *Natchez* did not arrive until six and a half hours later but the people gave her a great reception, too. Both captains were honored at a special dinner that evening, and everyone went home happy—except possibly Captain Leathers.

The great race showed America and the world that there was still lots of life left in Mississippi steamboating, and the great packets carried on for many more years. Gradually, however, the spreading railroad lines took away more and more of the steamboat passengers and freight. The grand side-wheelers gave way to stern-wheelers, and the number of boats grew smaller and smaller. Towboats soon outnumbered the passenger steamers, and great fleets of barges loaded with coal and other bulk cargoes could be seen being pushed along by stern-wheelers that resembled the old packets. It was found that such shipments could be made more cheaply by barge than by railroad, and in this way the steamboats were able to hold on to some of the freight business. Today these barge fleets can still be seen on the rivers. Some of them carry great numbers of new automobiles to the cities in the South. Occasionally a stern-wheeler will be seen pushing one of these tows, but most of the towboats have propellers with diesel engines providing the power.

There are just a handful of passenger steamboats left on the Mississippi, and most of them are used for short excursions. The side-wheeler *Admiral* at St. Louis is the biggest, but she does not resemble any of the old-time riverboats. Her superstructure is "streamlined," and from a distance she doesn't look like a steamboat at all. Another vessel, a fine big stern-wheeler called the *Delta Queen*, makes long cruises on the Mississippi, Ohio, and other rivers during the summer. She is the last steamboat left anywhere in the United States that carries overnight passengers. The *Delta Queen* is not a native of the Mississippi. She was built as a night boat in California to run between San Francisco and Sacramento and was in that service until the Government took her over in World War II. After the war she was towed around through the Panama Canal and all the way through the Gulf of Mexico to New Orleans. After being refitted, she became an adopted Mississippi steamboat, and she is now the best-known one on the western rivers.

STEAMBOATS ON THE INLAND SEAS

THE largest body of fresh water in all the world is Lake Superior, one of the Great Lakes separating the United States from Canada. Lake Superior is also the highest above sea level of the Great Lakes. Its waters at the eastern end flow into Lake Huron and Lake Michigan through the St. Marys River, cascading through a series of rapids at a place called Sault Ste. Marie. This is usually called the "Soo." At the other end of Lake Huron, the water flows into Lake Erie through the Detroit River and Lake St. Clair. Lake Erie is much higher than its neighbor to the east, Lake Ontario, and between the two the water thunders over the great falls of Niagara. From the eastern end of Ontario the lake water enters the St. Lawrence River, and after flowing hundreds of miles to the northeast, reaches the Atlantic Ocean near Newfoundland.

The St. Lawrence River was a "highway" for the French explorers and missionaries who came to North America soon after Columbus. At they moved westward they discovered the Great Lakes one by one, and used them to travel by canoe to the interior wilderness. Settlers followed the explorers, and after a time sails could be seen occasionally on the vast inland seas. Trappers and fur traders traveled throughout the area. It was many years before there were more than

The United States *was typical of the very early Great Lakes* steamboats. She carried sails in case the engines broke down.

a few little settlements along the Great Lakes. Not so on the St. Lawrence River. Many villages were established on its banks, and two of these, Montreal and Quebec, quickly grew into cities.

This was the way things were in the north country when Robert Fulton's first steamboat appeared on the Hudson. When news of this event reached Montreal the citizens of that city decided they would have to have a steamboat, too. Somehow plans were gotten together, and in 1809 a steamboat called the *Accommodation* was launched. She was very much like Robert Fulton's vessels, having a similar engine and side paddle wheels. In November she commenced running on the St. Lawrence. The *Accommodation* was not quite the first Canadian steamboat. Another vessel, called the *Dalhousie*, built at Prescott, Ontario, started running on the upper river just a short time before. Soon a small fleet of steamboats was running on the St. Lawrence, but it was not until 1817 that the splashing of paddle wheels was heard on Lake Ontario. First came the American steamboat *Ontario*, and she was followed within a couple of months by the Canadian steamer *Frontenac*. These were very flimsy vessels. Their builders apparently did not know what the big waves of a Lake Ontario storm could do even to a large craft. They soon found out. On one of her first trips the *Ontario* was caught in a heavy wind and she began to come apart. The paddle wheels broke loose from their bearings and jumped around, smashing the housings over them to bits. Shafts were bent and the engine was badly strained. The *Ontario* had to struggle back to port where she was rebuilt and made much stronger. After this experience the builders realized that steamboats for these great wild waters had to be solid, with lots of extra bracing and strong engines.

A year after the *Ontario* and *Frontenac* were launched the first steamboat appeared on Lake Erie. It was given the strange name *Walk-in-the-Water*. The story has been handed down that this came from a remark made by an Indian who used this expression to describe Robert Fulton's steamboat when he saw it on the Hudson. The name, however, seemed to be too long for most people. They just called her "the Steamboat."

Walk-in-the-Water was built on Robert Fulton's designs, and she turned out to be a fine steamboat. Her first long trip was west to Cleveland and Detroit, and she caused great excitement in those towns when she appeared. The Indians watched her steaming along in the distance with great interest. Some thought she was an evil spirit, others believed the steamboat was a great god who had gone over Niagara Falls long ago and was now returning.

For several years *Walk-in-the-Water* made regular trips back and forth along the south shore of Lake Erie until she met disaster. On the evening of November 1, 1821 she had left her home port of Black Rock, near Buffalo, and was heading out into the open lake. A storm was building up and things looked so bad that the captain decided to anchor near the shore. As night came on the wind howled, and the waves grew bigger and bigger. During the night *Walk-in-the-Water* broke loose from her anchor and was washed high up on the beach. The engineer jumped overboard, waded ashore, and roused the people living nearby. A crowd of rescuers collected, and they soon strung ropes to the steamer. By this means all the passengers and crew were saved. The steamboat became a total wreck, but her engine was not badly damaged. Later it was taken apart and hauled overland by oxen to be placed in a new steamboat, the *Superior*, which was then being built. This vessel operated on Lake Erie for many years, and when she was converted into a sailing craft in 1835, her secondhand engine went into still another steamboat, the *Charles Townsend*. So you see, even though the little *Walk-in-the-Water* had long since disappeared, her "spirit" went on and on.

New steamboats were built from time to time, but not nearly as many as on the Hudson or the Mississippi in those early days. By 1833 there were eleven running on the Lakes. Most of their trips were from Buffalo west, and a few boats even ventured 'way around to

R.N. Rice, *a favorite Great Lakes steamboat, was one of the early vessels of the Detroit and Cleveland Navigation Company.*

Chicago. A trip like that took about three weeks and was not made very often until bigger vessels were constructed. When the Erie Canal was built from the Hudson River to Lake Erie and Lake Ontario, the steamboat business began to grow faster. After the canal was finished in 1825 cargoes could be shipped all the way from Chicago to New York by water, but they had to be transferred from the lake steamers and sailing vessels to canal boats at Buffalo and Oswego. The canal boats were towed by mules across New York State to Albany. There a great many of them would be tied together, and then would be pulled by a steam towboat down the river to New York.

As time went on freight became even more important than passengers to the owners of Great Lakes steamboats. Vessels called "bulk carriers" were developed. These were driven by propellers and were really steamships rather than steamboats.

It wasn't until 1846 that a steamboat appeared on Lake Superior. A small side-wheeler called the *Independence* was hauled around the rapids at Sault Ste. Marie and launched into the biggest of all the Lakes. Other vessels were taken around in the same way later, but it was very hard work. In 1853 the State of Michigan began building a canal and locks to float vessels past the rapids. This great project was finished in 1855, and the first vessel to go through it into Lake Superior was the steamer *Illinois*. From that time on, the "Soo" locks carried great numbers of American and Canadian vessels day and night. Later, the Canadians built their own canal, but both have been open to the vessels of all countries.

The first steamboats on the Great Lakes did not have any upper decks. For a long time it was feared that any extra superstructure would make them top-heavy, and that the waves in big storms might roll them over. In 1839 the builders of a new steamboat called the *Great Western* decided to take a chance in adding extra cabins. Old-timers said this was dangerous, but it was found that the new vessel did not roll any worse than the others. Soon she was the most popular steamer on the lakes. Her engine was the high-pressure type like those used on the Mississippi steamboats. It was made in Pittsburgh, then taken apart and carried overland to Lake Erie.

When it was found that the *Great Western* was a safe vessel, builders began turning out bigger and bigger steamboats. Most of these were like the Hudson River boats of those days, but they were made heavier and had extra bracing to help them withstand the storms. Low-pressure walking-beam engines were preferred by the steamboat owners on the Lakes. Sometimes these would carry the figure of a galloping horse on top of the walking beam, and passengers thought that such a boat was extra fast.

In the 1850s hundreds of thousands of immigrants came to the United States from Europe. Most of them were poor people who wanted to have a new life in the great free country across the ocean. Some stayed in the crowded cities of the East, while others headed west to the wide-open spaces. The route from New York taken by most of the immigrants was up the Hudson by steamboat or railroad, then west by train or canal boat to Buffalo. There were so many people arriving at Buffalo that sometimes the Lake Erie steamboats could not carry them all. More boats were built, and rival vessels raced through the Lakes just as they did on the Hudson and the Mississippi.

Occasionally a big storm would catch some of the steamboats out in open water and they would go to the bottom with many lives lost. A few even disappeared without any trace and were never heard from again. There were also losses through fires, boiler explosions and collisions. One of these accidents occurred on the dark night of August 20, 1852 when the side-wheeler *Atlantic* was rammed by the propeller *Ogdensburg*. With a big gash cut in her hull, the *Atlantic* sank rapidly, and 131 people were drowned. Besides the passengers and a lot of cargo, the *Atlantic* was carrying a safe filled with money and gold belonging to an express company. Four years later, on a calm day,

Western World *was one of the greatest lake steamers of her day. She began running on Lake Erie in 1854 but was so costly to operate that she was soon laid up. Her paddle wheels were 39 feet in diameter.*

The Lake Michigan Steamboat Chicago, built in 1874. She ran for many years between Chicago and Milwaukee.

a diver wearing a suit of copper went down 160 feet to try to salvage the safe. He found everything on the steamer just as it was when she went down. According to newspaper accounts the diver claimed that as he landed on the *Atlantic's* deck he saw the figure of a woman standing upright with one hand holding onto a cable. She looked just as if she were alive, and as the water moved slightly her head nodded as if she were bowing to him. The bodies of other passengers were said to be about the steamer, all perfectly preserved. The diver found the safe, and it was hauled to the surface. The dead passengers, however, seem to have been left in their watery grave.

As the railroads pushed westward their lines began to encircle the Great Lakes, and they competed with the steamboats just as they had in the East. Several of them tried to capture the steamboat business by building boats of their own. In 1854 the Michigan Central Railroad launched two great side-wheelers named *Western World* and *Plymouth Rock*. When they appeared they were the biggest and most magnificent steamers ever seen on the Lakes. There were no finer vessels built for about 40 years. In fact, the *Western World* and *Plymouth Rock* proved to be too big and too expensive for the amount of trade available. In a short time the railroad tied them up at Detroit, where they stayed for six years without turning a wheel. In 1863 these fine steamers were towed to Buffalo and dismantled. Their engines were taken apart, shipped to New York and put into coastal steamers. The hulls became floating drydocks and were used to repair many smaller vessels.

The strangest of all craft on the Great Lakes came into being about 1890. These were the bulk cargo steamers called "whalebacks," invented by an engineer named Alexander McDougall. Whalebacks were built like great long floating tanks or pontoons. The smokestack, the pilothouse, and a little bit of cabin were the only things that appeared above the hull. All cargo was put below, and when the hatches were closed the waves could sweep right over one of these vessels without sinking her. All but one of the whalebacks were freighters. In 1892 a big passenger steamer was built on this design to run at Chicago during the Columbian Exposition. This vessel, called the *Christopher Columbus*, carried almost two million passengers during the season of 1893 on the six-mile trip from Jackson Park where the exposition was located to downtown Chicago. The *Christopher Columbus* had much

The Great Lakes steamer Seeandbee *was one of the largest side-wheelers ever built. She became a training aircraft carrier for the Navy in World War II and was called the* Wolverine. *After the war she was dismantled.*

The A. Wehrle, Jr. was one of a fleet of steamers running out of Sandusky and other ports at the western end of Lake Erie in the 1890s. The picture shows her at Cedar Point with all flags flying.

more deck housing above the hull than the freighter whalebacks, and she was designed so that she could unload five thousand passengers in five minutes. Visitors to the fair found the *Christopher Columbus* one of the main attractions, and she was a popular passenger carrier for many years afterward. It was not until 1936 that she was finally taken out of service and broken up.

All of the Great Lakes had passenger steamboats sailing through their waters until recent times. Most of the boats were of small or medium size. Lake Erie became the home of the giants, especially on the overnight trips from Buffalo to Cleveland and Detroit. The Cleveland and Buffalo Transit Company built the first of three monster steamboats in 1912. She was the *Seeandbee*, a side-wheeler 500 feet long—bigger than some of the ocean liners of those days. Biggest steamboat ever built up to that time, she was Queen of the Lakes until 1925. That year a different line, the Detroit and Cleveland Navigation Company, began running two side-wheelers that were even larger than the *Seeandbee*. These were called the *Greater Detroit* and the *Greater Buffalo*, and they were 536 feet long. They each had sleeping accommodations for 1,700 passengers and carried crews of 275. Their dining rooms had seats for 375 people. These huge steamboats, along with several others which were somewhat smaller, operated successfully until World War II. Then the U. S. Navy took over the *Seeandbee* and the *Greater Buffalo*, stripped them down, and turned them into training aircraft carriers. They were the first and only side-wheel aircraft carriers in history.

After the war the remaining giant, the *Greater Detroit*, and the other steamboats on Lake Erie drew fewer and fewer passengers. People were driving automobiles, and while they might like to look at the steamboats, they didn't bother to travel on them. One by one they went out of service, and now almost all are gone. There are still several passenger steamships on the Lakes running long cruises, but these are of a different type. The steamboats of the Inland Seas have passed into history.

The steamer Canadiana *carried summer excursionists between Buffalo, New York and Crystal Beach in Canada until just a few years ago.*

AROUND CAPE HORN BY STEAMBOAT

FOR many years after the first steamboats began running on the waters of the East Coast and on the Great Lakes and the Mississippi River system, there were none to be seen on the Pacific shores. There were hardly enough people in the scattered little settlements along the West Coast to attract more than an occasional sailing vessel. There was no way for a steamboat to travel from East to West without going all the way around South America, and this was so dangerous, even for a well-built sailing vessel, that the idea of taking a river boat on such a voyage was thought to be crazy.

However, when word came from California that gold had been discovered in the Sacramento Valley people quickly changed their minds about taking risks on the sea. You probably have heard the expression "people will do anything for money." Never was this more true than in the great Gold Rush of 1849–50. Hundreds left their homes, jobs and even their families in the East to set out for the Golden West. Many traveled in the great wagon trains overland, but most took the ocean route. In every port from Maine to Virginia sailing ships were advertised to take passengers for California, and all berths were quickly taken. There were not nearly enough vessels to handle all those who wanted to make the trip and many would-be gold miners had to wait weeks and even months before they could be on their way.

The Wilson G. Hunt, *a New York Harbor excursion steamboat, sailed all the way to San Francisco in the Gold Rush days. She served many years on the West Coast and made great amounts of money for her owners.*

It wasn't long before the owners of some of the smaller river and harbor steamboats began to see the chances of making a lot of money by sending their craft around to San Francisco, or Yerba Buena as it was formerly called. Not only could they collect a big fare from each of the hundred or more people who were willing to be packed aboard a steamboat, but also, when the voyage was finished the boat could be put into service on the Sacramento River carrying passengers to the gold fields. That is, if she didn't sink on the way out. Shipbuilders in New York, Boston and other eastern cities were kept busy boarding up windows and open decks, and strengthening steamboats as best they could for the long and dangerous trip.

Soon, one by one, a procession of old and new side-wheelers and a few propellers headed out into the stormy waters of the Atlantic, their holds loaded with all the coal they could carry. From New York went the Coney Island excursion boat *Wilson G. Hunt* and the side-wheel steamship *Senator*. The side-wheeler *Antelope* left her Delaware River service to go west. The New England coast steamboats *Commodore Preble*, *General Warren* and *W. J. Pease* headed out from Boston. On they went, their woodwork creaking and groaning as they rolled and pitched in the heavy seas. Some broke down or were damaged so badly by the ocean waves that they gave up and put into port even before they reached Florida. Others steamed on week after week, stopping only to take on coal and food. Down through the rough waters of the Straits of Magellan they went, then around into the Pacific. Finally, after months of steaming through storms and dangerous waters a few of them managed to reach San Francisco where their worn-out passengers were unloaded.

Not all the steamboats that went to California traveled under their own steam. A few like the Penobscot River stern-wheeler *Governor Dana* were taken apart, loaded on sailing ships and then put together again in San Francisco. A newly-built Canadian stern-wheeler, the *S. B. Wheeler*, was taken around the Horn piggy-back style. She was built at St. Stephen, New Brunswick about the same time as a sailing vessel called the *Fanny*. While crowds of people watched, the *Fanny* was sunk and the hull of the *S. B. Wheeler* was floated directly over her. Then the *Fanny* was pumped out and as she came up out of the

The famous steamer Senator *at Sacramento in the days of "gold fever." Men on the shore are assembling supplies to be taken to the "diggings." Note that both the steamer and the sailing vessel in front of her are tied to the stumps of old trees.*

water she lifted the steamboat right up with her. The *Wheeler*'s hull was lashed to the *Fanny*'s deck and her engine was stowed in the hold. Then off they sailed for the West. When San Francisco was reached the *Fanny* was again sunk and the *Wheeler* floated off.

One of the most famous eastern steamboats to make the trip to California during the gold rush was actually "stolen" by her captain. This was the fine side-wheeler *New World* built for William Brown of New York in 1850. Even before the *New World* was launched her owner found that he couldn't pay his bills, so his creditors filed a claim in the court that entitled them to hold the steamboat until the bills were paid. Mr. Brown thought for sure that he would lose his fine new vessel, but her captain, Edgar Wakeman, had other ideas. Wakeman was a sailing ship man who decided to go into steamboating. He saw the *New World* on the launching ways at the shipyard and decided that she was the boat he wanted to command. He called on Mr. Brown who hired him very quickly because of his experience. Captain Wakeman did not know at first that Mr. Brown was in financial trouble and that the *New World* might be taken away from him. As soon as he heard the bad news, however, he began to make plans to get around the sheriff and his deputies. First thing was to get the steamboat launched. The sheriff agreed to this, since he would have just as much control over the vessel in the water as on land—or so he thought.

It was the cold Sunday morning of February 10, 1850 when the *New World* slid down the ways—with steam up in her boilers! She is said to have been the first steamboat ever launched with a "hot" engine and this made the sheriff's men very suspicious. Captain Wakeman told them he wanted to work the rust off the engine, and persuaded them to let him make a trial trip. Since they would stay on board with their trusty revolvers, the lawmen agreed. Besides, the captain had provided baskets of champagne and it was warm in the main saloon. While the deputies drank and sat with their feet on the furniture, the *New World* proved that she was a fast, able steamboat. Captain Wakeman was pleased, and he brought the vessel back to her dock just before midnight. By that time the sheriff's men were quite drunk from champagne and some of them were snoring.

Next day Captain Wakeman told his employer, Mr. Brown, what he had in mind. It was his plan to sail the *New World* all the way to California and the gold fields. There she would make a lot of money carrying passengers on the Sacramento River, and Mr. Brown would then be able to pay his debts. At first Mr. Brown thought the captain was out of his mind, but then the idea began to look good to him. After all, he had very little to lose and Captain Wakeman was a man to be trusted. Finally he agreed to the scheme. The captain talked the sheriff into letting him put more coal aboard "to turn the engines over once in awhile," and he secretly hired a crew for the long voyage. The men sneaked aboard after dark one night while the deputies sat in the saloon drinking the liquor the captain had thoughtfully provided. In fact, for several days they had such a fine time drinking and snoozing they didn't even notice all the supplies and the coal that went into the hold of the *New World*.

Captain Wakeman had decided to sail on Saturday, February 16th, but engine trouble developed and he had to wait until the next day. Meanwhile, the sheriff's office had begun to hear rumors, and they became more watchful. Undersheriff Cunningham personally took charge

The old Pacific Coast steamboat Goliah *started life as a New York Harbor towboat. In April 1850 she sailed around the Horn to San Francisco and became a passenger boat on the Sacramento River. Later she was rebuilt as a coastal steamboat and was called the* Defender. *Finally she again became a towboat with her old name and served many years on Puget Sound.*

of the men on board the steamboat Saturday night and he warned Captain Wakeman not to pull any tricks. Next morning, just one week after the *New World*'s launching, she took off on another "rust-removing" cruise about New York Harbor. Undersheriff Cunningham several times ordered the steamer back to her dock. When she headed down the "Narrows" and out toward the sea the lawmen really became alarmed. Cunningham drew his pistol, and grabbing Captain Wakeman by the collar, ordered him to turn the vessel around and head back. In seconds the unhappy undersheriff was surrounded by the steamer's crew all armed with knives and cutlasses. Cunningham surrendered along with his deputies and they were rowed ashore and dumped on the beach at Staten Island. Before they had waded out of the mud and climbed up onto high ground the *New World* was well on her way out to sea.

All that night she rolled and pitched in a big gale and her superstructure was damaged. However, the next morning the sea calmed down and the steamboat headed down the coast to Pernambuco, Brazil. There she stopped a short time for coal and supplies and was soon at sea again. Near Rio de Janeiro she was fired upon and chased by a British warship, but being much more speedy, she was able to get away and head into Rio Harbor. The forts on shore, having heard the cannonading at sea, thought the *New World* was an invader. They also fired at her, but she dodged their cannon balls and anchored near an American warship that happened to be in the harbor. The Brazilian Customs men demanded to see the steamboat's papers, but Captain Wakeman knew that was impossible. They were in the hands of the sheriff at New York. The captain took the tin box that would have held the papers and put some pieces of chain in it. Then he had a couple of his crewmen row him to the dock where a large crowd stood watching. Right in front of everybody he pretended to lose his balance and fell overboard with a big splash. Of course the tin box containing the "papers" sank and was not recovered. Captain Wakeman headed right to the U. S. Consul and told him of the bad luck he'd had. The Consul immediately prepared new papers, the first on board the *New World* since she had sailed from New York.

Captain Wakeman wanted to have the *New World* put into drydock immediately because she was leaking badly. Brazilian officials told him the steamer would have to be quarantined for thirty days before they could do anything. The Captain raised such a fuss that the matter soon came to the attention of the Emperor of Brazil. He became so annoyed that he sent word to the Royal drydocks to repair the American steamboat as fast as possible so she could get out of his country. Captain Wakeman and his crew were all in favor. In fact, they feared having to stay in Rio even long enough for the necessary repairs. The city was in the grip of a terrible yellow fever epidemic and people were dying by the hundreds. Soon the disease spread to the crew of the *New World* and 18 men died in a very short time. Captain Wakeman had to find replacements in order to continue the voyage. Finally they were under way again with a crew that was largely inexperienced and then two more died on board including the mate. However, the steamboat paddled on and on. Down around the tip of South America she steamed, through the Straits of Magellan and out into the Pacific. At Panama Captain Wakeman was almost arrested by two U. S. Marshals, but he managed to frighten them off. The *New World* took on over two hundred passengers there who had crossed the Isthmus from the east side. Of course, the Panama Canal did not exist in those days.

Finally, after more adventures and near disaster in a bad Pacific Ocean storm, Captain Wakeman brought the *New World* into San Francisco Bay with flags flying five months after she had left New

York. The harbor was quite a sight. Hundreds and hundreds of sailing ships lined the shores and many more were anchored out in the Bay. Most of them had been abandoned by their crews who had rushed off to the gold diggings. The scene was described as a "forest of masts," and it is likely that at no other time were there so many ships clustered together at one time in a single bay. Most of them stayed there until they finally sank and the growing city covered them with sand and dirt to make more land.

While the sailing ships were finished with their job, the steamboats were not. The *New World* soon joined a growing fleet running from San Francisco to Sacramento on the Sacramento River, and to Stockton on the San Joaquin River. Long after the Gold Rush had ended those early steamboats continued to sail the Bay and the many rivers that flowed into it.

HE first voyage of a steam vessel to the West Coast of North America began, of all places, in England. In 1835 a little paddle wheel steamship called the *Beaver* left her birthplace on the Thames River near London, and sailed away for the Pacific. To say that she sailed was correct in this instance, because her side wheels had been taken off and stowed on deck. She was rigged as a sailing vessel for the long voyage, and her engine did not turn over once until after she had arrived at the Columbia River 163 days later. One hundred fifty thousand British subjects, led by King William, went to the Thames to see the *Beaver* sail, and all England thought it was wonderful when the news finally came back that she had reached her destination.

There were not many settlers on the coast in those days. The fur trade was important, and it was for this that the little *Beaver* had been built. She was owned by the Hudson's Bay Company which had trading posts all through Canada. For almost fourteen years the *Beaver* had only sailing ships for company as she paddled along the northwest coast.

Farther south, in the territory of California, the wide waters of San Francisco Bay had not yet seen a steamboat. In fact, there were very few vessels of any kind stopping there because there were hardly any people living on the shores. Then one day in 1847 a Russian sailing ship dropped anchor in the harbor to deliver some goods and a steamboat. This little craft, all in pieces, was only 37 feet long—hardly more than a launch. She had been running in Alaska, and a local merchant had bought her for use on the Bay.

As we have seen, the discovery of gold quickly brought many changes to San Francisco and the entire West Coast. In 1853 a steamboat called the *Shasta* was launched at San Francisco, and she was the first to be built in the West. Dozens of others appeared after her. Some were side-wheelers, others were stern-wheelers or propellers. Quite a few in the early days had come around the Horn from the East Coast and their design had an influence on the side-wheelers that were built on the West Coast later. Some of the stern-wheelers were built by men from the middle western rivers and these vessels looked like Mississippi boats. Finally, a whole new style of steamboat came to be seen on the western shores of our country, and these vessels had a bit of the Hudson and a bit of the Mississippi combined in them. They increased in number rapidly and spread from San Francisco Bay to Puget Sound in Washington, to the Columbia River and its tributaries, to the lakes and rivers of British Columbia and to Alaskan waterways.

Double-ended ferryboats like the ones in New York Harbor began running on San Francisco Bay and soon there was no place in the world that had more of these big "floating bridges." Most of the San Francisco ferries were side-wheelers and one, the *Newark*, had huge

The ferryboat Newark *was typical of the big side-wheelers that linked San Francisco with other cities on the Bay.*

A stern-wheeler in the wild and rocky waters of the upper Columbia River.

paddle boxes over the wheels that rose higher than the top deck. Two side-wheelers, the *Solano* and the *Contra Costa*, were built to carry whole railroad trains across Carquinez Strait. These were the largest double-ended ferryboats ever built and they ran until the Southern Pacific Railroad built a bridge to take their place.

The adventures of steamboats and steamboatmen on the West Coast have been told in many fine books. One of the most exciting stories is about the trip of the stern-wheel steamer *Shoshone* down the wild canyon of the Snake River. She had been built on the upper branches of that river at Fort Boise, Idaho to serve the mining camps in the area. Her timbers were cut by hand, and the iron used in making her engines was carried hundreds of miles on the backs of mules

and pack horses. She was truly a wilderness steamboat, but her owners expected to make a lot of money with her in carrying miners to
the Idaho gold fields. Before she was finished, however, a new and
easier route to the mines was discovered. The *Shoshone* had no place
to run, so for some time she was tied up in a lonely spot far from
civilization.

The company that owned her decided to try to bring her down
the Snake River to the Columbia where she could be used. The first
crew sent out brought her down the river as far as a place called Lime
Point, then gave up. Below that point there was a deep canyon with
raging rapids and big sharp rocks. It looked as though it would be an
impossible job to get the *Shoshone* through. The company finally found
two men who were willing to take the risks and they were ordered to
bring her through or wreck her in the attempt. The two, Captain
Sebastian Miller and Chief Engineer Daniel Buchanan, had to travel
from Portland, Oregon on buckboards, sleds, wagons, on horseback and
on foot to reach the place where the *Shoshone* was tied up. It took them
more than three weeks to get there. The steamer was made ready, the
boilers were fired up, and down the roaring river she went.

The plan was to keep her stern wheel turning in reverse as if
she were trying to back up the river against the current. This gave the
pilot some control, but when the *Shoshone* hit the first bad set of rapids
the paddle wheel became damaged and wasn't of any more use. The
steamer swung around in whirlpools, banged against big rocks, and
nearly tipped over several times. In one crash about eight feet of her

bow was knocked off, and she lost her forward flagpole. This was carried downstream far ahead of the steamer, and when it reached the lower river people saw it and thought the *Shoshone* had been wrecked. They underestimated Captain Miller and Engineer Buchanan, however. Somehow they managed to get the steamer through each series of rapids without great damage. In between they tied up to the bank to make temporary repairs and to rest. At one place the steamer had to pass through a narrow gorge with walls of solid rock. The roar of the rushing water was so loud that it drowned out all other noise. The spray was so thick that at times it almost hid the *Shoshone* from view. As she plunged on, her bow dipped under the surface several times and tons of water poured into her hold. The firemen had to rush out on deck to avoid being drowned. On April 27th the *Shoshone* shot through the last of the rapids and arrived at Lewiston, Idaho. As she came about to make a landing, Captain Miller shouted through the speaking tube from the pilothouse to the engine room, "I say, Buck, I expect if this company wanted a couple of men to take a steamboat through hell, they would send for you and me."

On June 29th the *Shoshone* was taken over another falls and on down the Columbia River to a place called The Dalles in Oregon. The *Shoshone* was put in drydock and a great deal of repair work was done to put her in good condition again. After all the effort to get her down to civilization and into service you'd think that she would have been put to work carrying first-class passengers, at least. But no, her owners decided she would make a fine cattle boat, and for several years she ran up and down the middle part of the Columbia loaded with bellowing steers and mooing cows. In 1873 she was piloted over one more set of rapids, the great Cascades at The Dalles, and taken to the Willamette River, a large tributary of the Columbia. The City of Portland is near its lower end.

After one year on the Willamette the *Shoshone* struck a rock and sank. It was found that she couldn't be raised so her engines were taken out and the hull left to fall apart. With a rise in the river, the remains of the poor old steamboat floated down to a place called Lincoln. Here a farmer took possession of her and made a big chicken-house out of the superstructure.

Only one other steamboat went down through the Snake River canyons after the *Shoshone*'s safe trip. This was a stern-wheeler called the *Norma*, which navigated the treacherous river 25 years after the *Shoshone* had proved that it could be done.

The Pacific Slope, as the Far West is called, rises quite steeply as it approaches the great mountain ranges that run from Canada almost to the border of Mexico. Almost all of the many rivers that flow into the great Columbia have roaring waterfalls and rapids. In spite of the fact that this made navigation by steamboats extra diffi-cult, it did not stop the hardy mariners of those olden days. Vessels were taken up through rapids and down again. There was hardly a mile of river deep enough to float a steamboat that didn't have one or more of them on it. Builders experimented with different types of vessels hoping to find one that would be best for the wild rushing rivers, but

Puget Sound steamer Olympian *ashore in the Straits of Magellan at the southern tip of South America. While being towed to New York by the steamship* Zealandia, *she broke loose in a storm and was washed up on the beach. You can still see parts of her engine today if you travel to that distant and desolate shore.*

they never did agree on a single design that worked best. Many of the upper river steamboats were quite small and some were very strange in their appearance. For example, there was the *Skedaddle*, a type of vessel called a steam barge. She was built to run on the Willamette River and spent her career there. She must have been put together in a very flimsy way because the steamboat inspectors would not let her come down to the mouth of the Willamette where it joins the Columbia. Another odd steamboat was the *Hoosier No. 3*, a small side-wheeler also built for service on the Willamette. This vessel's engines were connected to the paddle wheel shafts by a lot of noisy gears. Old-timers said that you could hear her grinding and clanking long after she had passed by.

In the Far West, as in other parts of the country, steamboatmen had troubles with the Indians. Up through the middle of the nineteenth century tribes roamed the countryside, pouncing on unprotected villages and killing many settlers. For a period of time in the 1850s the Indians took to shooting at steamboats from the riverbanks. Passengers often had to "hit the deck" fast or run inside the cabins to get away from the hail of bullets. Finally, the Army moved in with troops and the undeclared war was ended.

Two Columbia River stern-wheelers in the Cascade Locks. The large steamboat is the famous Bailey Gatzert. *The other is the* Dalles City.

Steamboats of the northwestern rivers had their share of boiler explosions and other accidents. Many of these were serious and caused loss of life. Several had very odd consequences. There was the time, for instance, when the steamer *Elk* blew up on the Willamette. The blast was so powerful that most of the steamer's deckhouse went up in the air. Captain George Jerome was blown so high that he landed in the top of a big cottonwood tree on the way down. Neither he nor any of the passengers or crew was killed, although some were hurt. Captain Jerome's tree became famous and for years afterward captains of passing steamboats would point it out to their passengers.

Toward the end of the nineteenth century many fine fast steamboats appeared on the lower Columbia River. The graceful *Telephone*, launched in 1884, was said to be the fastest stern-wheel steamboat in the world. She sometimes raced with the larger side-wheeler

Alaskan and was usually able to keep up with her powerful rival. The *Telephone* burned down to her hull in 1887, but she had been such a successful steamboat that Captain Scott, her owner, decided to rebuild her. The following year she appeared as a new steamer but with the same name she had carried before the fire. Like the *Telephone*, most stern-wheel steamers of the Columbia were long and graceful, with tall slim smokestacks and covered paddle wheels.

There were many fine side-wheelers on the Columbia River, too. One of the most famous of these in later years was the *T. J. Potter*. She was said to have had a hull modeled after the fast Hudson River steamboat *Daniel Drew*, and there were not many steamboats in the West that could make better speed.

The mouth of the Columbia River on the coast of Oregon and Washington is about 150 miles south of the Strait of Juan de Fuca. This wide waterway divides the State of Washington from Vancouver Island in Canada, and it is the entrance to the great body of water which includes Puget Sound and the Strait of Georgia. This is almost like an inland sea, and in the old days its surface would be alive with steamboats going in all directions. Even today you can see many vessels from both Canada and the United States steaming from port to port in the area.

Puget Sound, since the days of the early settlers, has been one of the most important waterways in North America, and over the years it has floated hundreds of steamboats, big and little. First was the Hudson's Bay Company steamer *Beaver*, mentioned earlier. The

Beaver ranged up and down the coast in the fur trade, and sailed in and out of the Sound from time to time. The first regular Puget Sound steamboats were built in the East and either sailed around the Horn under their own steam or were shipped in pieces aboard sailing vessels. Service between Olympia, Washington and Vancouver, British Columbia was started by the little propeller *Major Tompkins*, and she was followed by the *Traveler* and the *Daniel Webster*. All of these steamboats were small and slow, and they were soon replaced by bigger and better ones. Quite a few of the vessels from San Francisco Bay came north to try their luck on new routes. Among them were our old friends from New York, the *Wilson G. Hunt* and the *New World*. Competition was very tough and some steamboat owners lost a great deal of money instead of becoming rich as they had hoped.

The graceful stern-wheeler Telephone was a favorite on the Columbia River and Puget Sound. Said to be the fastest stern-wheeler in the world, she burned to the water's edge and was completely rebuilt in 1887.

One of the greatest battlers in the steamboat wars for many years was a vessel called the *Eliza Anderson*. This remarkable side-wheeler was said to have run slower and made money faster than any steamboat in the Northwest. She was built at Portland and ran on or near Puget Sound for nearly 40 years. There are many stories about the *Eliza Anderson's* experiences. Steamboat after steamboat was put into direct competition with her, but they were almost all forced to quit. One time a rival vessel, the *George E. Starr*, came a little too close to the "old lady" after they had both gone into a patch of fog. A little while later one steamboat emerged from the mist and went on her way. It was the *Eliza Anderson*. She had rammed the *George E. Starr*, leaving her disabled and wallowing in the fog bank, while her captain cursed a blue streak. Several times the *Anderson* was laid up for what many people thought was the last time, but she always came back. In 1897 with the Alaska gold rush in full swing, the *Eliza Anderson* took off with a full load of passengers for the northland. A bad storm blew her ashore at Dutch Harbor in the Aleutian Islands. Her passengers and crew got off safely, but the old steamer became a total wreck.

Puget Sound has seen many great steamboats of all types. There were big side-wheelers like the *Alaskan*, *Olympian* and the *Yosemite*. Among the famous stern-wheelers were the beautiful *Bailey Gatzert*, the low, slim *Greyhound*, the *Telegraph* and the *Telephone*. There were even more well-known steamers in the propeller class, including the *Flyer*, the *Tacoma*, the *H. B. Kennedy*, and the Canadian steamers *Joan* and *Princess Victoria*. Two famous propellers, the *Indi-*

anapolis and the *Iroquois* came to Puget Sound all the way from the Great Lakes. Their voyage included a trip through the Panama Canal. From the Hudson came the fine propeller *City of Kingston*.

Puget Sound also has been the home of one of the largest ferry fleets in the world. Originally there were side-wheel ferryboats, but these soon gave way to propellers. Finally, steam engines all but disappeared and diesels took their place. The first large, completely streamlined vessel in the world was a Puget Sound ferryboat, the *Kalakala*.

It is interesting to think that a great deal of the steamboat business on the West Coast developed because of "gold fever." We have seen how the California Gold Rush of 1849 brought men and steamboats from the East. Later gold discoveries were made on the Fraser River in British Columbia, and in Idaho and western Montana. In each case steamboats were rushed into service to help the miners travel to the gold fields, and to carry needed supplies. California gold was discovered on the land of a settler named John Sutter, who had a mill and a fort near what is now the city of Sacramento. This was a fairly easy point to reach by steamboat, and in the course of a few months there was a growing fleet sailing from San Francisco to the gold fields. The route was northeast across the bay to Carquinez Strait, then into Suisun Bay and on up the Sacramento River. Pioneers settled all along the river valley, and many of them became farmers, raising fruits and vegetables. The Gold Rush died out in a few years, but by that time the steamboats were kept busy with other things. Gradually the old worn-out eastern vessels like the *Wilson G. Hunt*, the *Antelope*, and the *New World* were replaced by newer California-built steamboats. Big side-wheelers like the *Capital* and the *Yosemite* appeared on the river. In 1860 the most famous and beautiful of all the Sacramento steamboats was launched. She was called the *Chrysopolis*, which means Golden City, and she was queen of the river for 15 years. In 1875 she was bought by the Central Pacific Railroad to be converted into a ferryboat, and in the spring of that year she appeared, completely re-built, as the *Oakland*. For another 75 years or so she carried passengers and vehicles across the bay from the San Francisco docks to the railroad terminal at Oakland.

When the great bridge from San Francisco to Oakland was finished just before World War II only a couple of railroad ferryboats were kept in service. The old *Oakland* was sold to a marine junk dealer who began the big job of taking her apart in January 1940. All went well until sparks from an acetylene torch started a fire. In a short time the old river queen turned ferryboat became a roaring blaze that threatened docks and vessels along the Oakland waterfront. It took several fire companies and a fireboat to get things under control. The old *Chrysopolis* had really gone out in a blaze of glory.

The Sacramento and San Joaquin rivers became famous for their great fleets of stern-wheel steamboats which carried freight and passengers right up to the time of World War II. Farmers and ranchers along the rivers depended on the steamers to carry their products to market. Smaller vessels, given over mostly to freight, would make dozens of landings on their regular trips.

As late as 1926 the California Steam Navigation Company, operator of most of the riverboats, built two fine big stern-wheel night boats, the *Delta King* and the *Delta Queen*. Their steel hulls were built in Scotland, shipped over in pieces and reassembled in a California shipyard. The *King* and *Queen* were probably the finest stern-wheelers ever built, but they came to the Sacramento too late. By the time they began running, automobiles and trucks were rapidly taking the passengers and freight away.

In 1941 the *King* and *Queen* were laid up and the sad word was spread that they would never again sail the bay and river they had served so well. It was thought for a time that the *Queen* would be sent east for service on the Hudson, but before arrangements could be worked out, both she and her sister ship were taken by the Government for use in the war effort. The *King* finally was sent to Alaska and there became a barracks, but the *Queen*, as mentioned earlier, began a whole new career as a cruise steamboat on the Mississippi. The passing of the *Delta Queen* would mark the end of a long history of steamboats that sailed on San Francisco Bay and the rivers that flow into it.

As we said earlier, there are many fine books that have been published about steamboating in all parts of the country. Some are hard to find because they've been out of print for many years. If you are interested, try your local library. A list of such books follows. Most were used as reference in compiling this history, and the author acknowledges the help received from these other writers who set forth many interesting incidents that might otherwise not be known.

Sunrise on San Francisco Bay many years ago. One of the big Sacramento River steamboats is seen approaching her landing.

BIBLIOGRAPHY

ALBION, ROBERT GREENHALGH. *The Rise of New York Port, 1815-1860.* New York: C. Scribner's, 1939.

BARKHAU, ROY L. *The Great Steamboat Race Between the Natchez and the Robert E. Lee.* (paper cover booklet) Cincinnati, Ohio: The Picture Publishing Company, 1925. A complete, well written story of the most famous steamboat race of all time.

BROWN, ALEXANDER CROSBY. *The Old Bay Line.* Richmond, Virginia: The Dietz Press, 1940.

BUCKMAN, DAVID LEAR. *Old Steamboat Days on the Hudson.* New York: Grafton Historical Press, 1907.

BURGESS, ROBERT H. AND H. GRAHAM WOODS. *Steamboats Out of Baltimore.* Cambridge, Maryland: Tidewater Publishers, 1968.

COLDEN, CADWALLADER D. *The Life of Robert Fulton.* New York: Kirk & Mercein, 1817. Written by a distinguished New Yorker and friend of the inventor.

COVELL, WILLIAM KING. *A Short History of the Fall River Line.* Newport, Rhode Island: A. Hartley G. Ward, 1947.

DUNBAR, SEYMOUR. *History of Travel in America.* Indianapolis: Bobbs-Merrill Company, 1915. (Four volumes) A complete treatise on this subject from earliest times. Well illustrated.

DUNBAUGH, EDWIN L. *The Era of the Joy Line: a Saga of Steamboating on Long Island Sound.* Westport, Connecticut: Greenwood Press, 1982.

EWEN, WILLIAM H. "The Hudson's Blackest Day," *Yonkers Historical Society Bulletin*, July 1965. Article on the burning of the *Henry Clay.*

GOULD, EMERSON W. *Fifty Years on the Mississippi.* St. Louis: Nixon-Jones Printing Co., 1889. [Reprinted in 1951] A miscellaneous compendium of events on the western rivers from earliest times.

HANSON, JOSEPH MILLS. *The Conquest of the Missouri.* Chicago, 1909. [Reprint by Rinehart & Company, 1946] The life and exploits of Captain Grant Marsh.

HILTON, GEORGE W. *The Night Boat.* Berkeley, California: Howell-North Books, 1968.

HUNTER, LOUIS C. *Steamboats on the Western Rivers.* Cambridge: Harvard University Press, 1949. Probably the most accurate and complete study of the steamboat era on the Mississippi and its tributaries.

KEMBLE, JOHN HASKELL. *San Francisco Bay, A Pictorial Maritime History.* Cambridge, Maryland: Cornell Maritime Press, 1957.

LASS, WILLIAM E. *A History of Steamboating on the Upper Missouri River.* Lincoln, Nebraska: University of Nebraska Press, 1962. A well documented history of steamboating on the "Big Muddy" from pioneer days.

LATROBE, JOHN H. B. *The First Steamboat Voyage on the Western Waters.* [Baltimore, Maryland]: The Maryland Historical Society, 1871. Description of the trip of Fulton's steamboat *New Orleans* down the Ohio and Mississippi rivers.

MCADAM, ROGER WILLIAMS. *The Old Fall River Line.* New York: Stephen Daye Press, 1937, 1955. Colorful description of the development of this great line, and its sad ending. Much written from the author's personal experience.

MILLS, JAMES COOKE. *Our Inland Seas, Their Shipping & Commerce for Three Centuries.* Chicago: A. C. McClurg & Company, 1910.

MORRISON, JOHN H. *History of American Steam Navigation.* New York: W. F. Sametz & Company, 1903; revision, New York: Stephen Daye Press, 1958.

NEWELL, GORDON AND JOE WILLIAMSON. *Pacific Steamboats.* Seattle: Superior Publishing Company, 1958.

NEWELL, GORDON R. *Pacific Coastal Liners.* Seattle: Superior Publishing Company, 1959.

PREBLE, GEORGE HENRY. *A Chronological History of the Origin and Development of Steam Navigation, 1543-1882.* Philadelphia: L. R. Hamersly, 1883.

QUICK, HERBERT. *Mississippi Steamboatin'; a History of Steamboating on the Mississippi and its Tributaries.* New York: H. Holt and Company, 1926.

RINGWALD, DONALD C. *Hudson River Day Line, The Story of a Great Steamboat Company.* Berkeley, California: Howell-North Books, 1965.

WAKEMAN, EDGAR. *Log of an Ancient Mariner, Being the Life and Adventures of Captain Edgar Wakeman.* San Francisco: A. L. Bancroft & Company, 1878.

WAY, FREDERICK. *Pilotin' Comes Natural.* New York: Farrar & Rinehart, 1943.

WAY, FREDERICK. *Log of the Betsy Ann.* New York: R. M. McBride & Company, 1933.

WRIGHT, E. W., EDITOR. *Lewis & Dryden's Marine History of the Pacific Northwest.* Portland, Oregon: Lewis & Dryden Printing Company, 1895.

INDEX

(Italicized numbers indicate illustrations)

PICTURE CREDITS

Cover   From a painting by J. G. Tyler, The Eldredge Collection, courtesy The Mariners' Museum, Newport News, Virginia

Half Title   Courtesy The Mariners' Museum

Frontispiece, 6, 9, 11, 12, 17, 33, 43, 51, 54, 56, 65, 76, 80, 82, 101, 107 From the author's collection

8   S. W. Stanton, *American Steam Vessels*

13   *Transactions of the Institute of Naval Architects*, London 1861

14   Photo by Mary Anne Stets

15   Photo by Edward O. Clark

19   S. W. Stanton, *American Steam Vessels*

20   From a drawing by the author

26   Lithograph after painting by Karl *(sic)* Bodmer, courtesy The Mariners' Museum

37   Eldredge Collection, courtesy The Mariners' Museum

38   Eldredge Collection, courtesy The Mariners' Museum

40   Eldredge Collection, courtesy The Mariners' Museum

45   Photo by William King Covell

46   Andrew Fletcher; from a paper on River, Lake, Bay and Sound Steamboats of the United States, International Engineering Congress, San Francisco 1915

60   Steamboat Photo Service

63   S. W. Stanton, *American Steam Vessels*

66   Steamboat Photo Service

69   Steamboat Photo Service

73   Courtesy New York Public Library

81   The Detroit Publishing Company

83   Photo by Frederick C. Shipley

85   Courtesy The Mariners' Museum

87   Courtesy New York Public Library

90   S. W. Stanton, *American Steam Vessels*

95   Clark Collection, courtesy Peabody Museum, Salem, Mass.

96   Courtesy Oregon Historical Society

100   Dunbaugh Collection, courtesy Steamship Historical Society of America

103   Courtesy Oregon Historical Society